ANATOMY
of a
SUCCESSFUL
SALESMAN

ANATOMY
of a
SUCCESSFUL
SALESMAN

Arthur Mortell

FARNSWORTH PUBLISHING COMPANY, INC.
Rockville Centre, N.Y.

CONTENTS

I	What Determines Success	9
II	Attitudes toward Failure	23
III	Anxiety and Creative Energy	33
IV	Ego Defense Mechanisms	45
V	The Challenge to Change	57
VI	Self-image Psychology	69
VII	The Anatomy of Personality	77
VIII	Twelve Goal-achieving Techniques	87
IX	Twelve More Goal-achieving Techniques	101
X	A Workshop Section	111
XI	Alpha-level Conditioning	117
XII	Alpha-level Techniques	131
XIII	On Interpersonal Relations	141
XIV	The Psychology of Rapport	151
XV	Consumer Motivation	161
XVI	The Psychology of Persuasion	169
XVII	Techniques of Persuasion	175
XVIII	Leadership	187
XIX	It Is Your Responsibility	199

FOREWORD

Art Mortell has written a distinctively different kind of book for salesmen. Rather than cover the well-trodden path on the techniques for engineering agreement, Mr. Mortell deals with the problems of negative self-image and the fear of rejection that can hamper personal growth and achievement.

As Shakespeare said in Act 1, Scene 2, of Julius Caesar, ". . . The fault, dear Brutus, is not in our stars but in ourselves . . ." Self awareness is essential to the discovery of inner strengths that allow individuals to achieve beyond their previously self-limiting assessments.

This book provides a valuable self-help program for salesmen. By coming to grips with reality and gaining a new appreciation of his capabilities, one can set for himself challenging goals which he now believes he can attain. Through a process of greater self-awareness and self-appreciation, the salesman, by using Mr. Mortell's guidelines, can become not only more effective and more productive, but a happier, better-adjusted person as well.

HERBERT D. EAGLE *President*
Sales and Marketing Executives International

PREFACE

This book owes its existence to a decision I made in 1961 while finishing my Bachelors Degree in Social Science at Pace College (New York). I intended to become a social worker, but after exploring the income opportunities and appraising my own obligations and objectives, decided to seek instead a career as a salesman which seemed to offer both financial rewards and personal satisfaction.

I applied to IBM and was turned down, so became the Asst. V.P. of Sales for Old Town Corporation, working primarily in sales promotion. My work in trade shows, demonstrating the Old Town line of office supplies, interested me to the extent that I convinced the company to give me a try at selling.

On a test basis I called on businesses in the Williamsburg Savings Bank Building in Brooklyn and was turned down nineteen times in the first two hours. It is difficult to describe the depression I felt on the two-mile walk back to the office, as I realized I would never be a salesman. No one had bought from me.

A couple of weeks later I came across my notes of that negative day and, in reviewing them, discovered that two people had actually requested samples. I had been so discouraged by the seventeen negative responses that I was never consciously aware of any successes. I delivered the samples, making a point to call on no one else, and made one sale. I then realized that success was a matter of percentages. A few weeks later, in 1962, I began selling on Wall Street for Old Town. In 1963 I applied again at IBM, was hired, and sold seventy new accounts for the typewriter division in a ten-month period.

Concurrent with my work, I was finishing my Masters Degree in Marketing Management with my thesis in Salesmanship. I reviewed almost one hundred books and articles in an effort to find material that would surpass my IBM training, without success until I started working with the insurance industry. With its wealth of experience in sales training and work, and its utter dependence upon its ability to market an intangible product which meets great sales resistance, the insurance industry went significantly beyond the existing material I had already researched.

When I finished my thesis I had a composite of the most advanced techniques in persuasion, but some thoughts troubled me: "If the insurance industry has such a fine training program, why do they still have a 62% turnover in the first year? How was it that you could furnish the greatest technical and selling ideas to ten young, personable individuals and in three years eight or nine would fail? What do you find in the successful salesman that is missing in most others?"

Nor is the insurance industry unusual in this respect. An evaluation of other industries shows similar percentages of failures, not only in salesmanship but in virtually all areas of effort. For example, for each 100 businesses just getting started, only six will succeed. Approximately 220 companies go bankrupt in this country each week.

Why do some salesmen succeed while others fail? What determines the make-up of the successful individual? Is it possible that some are programmed for failure and others for success? The following year I had an opportunity to explore these questions. I moved to California and began teaching at night at Pasadena College while still selling for IBM. By 1967, I felt I had some answers and began giving seminars in the evening. One stockbroker earning $2,000 per month doubled his income and could explain how the seminar had helped him. With this success I began giving seminars full time in the summer of 1968—my work with salesmen since then has become the basis for The Anatomy of a Successful Salesman. I would like to think that you will have the same success in applying the concepts in this book as have so many others with whom I have worked in recent years.

I

What Determines Success

History tells us that in each age there were men of imagination who saw a goal no one else could see and who fought valiantly to achieve that goal, even in the face of countless failures. Without them there would have been no progress—only a static society. What were the characteristics of such men, that they were able to reach levels of success which most people never begin to imagine?

A Time of Change

Before discussing what determines success, I would like you to take a trip back in time. It is December 17, 1903, and the Wright brothers are at Kitty Hawk. It is a cold day, and puddles of water from recent rain have turned to ice. A flimsy object of wood, wire, and cloth is being readied for a great attempt: Man is going to try the impossible—to fly. Imagine the excitement of these men as this first airplane travels the distance of 120 feet in twelve seconds.

It is now sixty-six years later and the Apollo 11 sits on top of a Saturn Five rocket. It is 60 feet taller than the Statue of Liberty and thirteen times heavier. Moments later it moves into the sky, gradually increasing speed, until it is traveling 25,000 miles per hour, 400 miles per minute. We live in a period of great technological change where, in a seventy-year period, we have traveled from Kitty Hawk to the moon.

Since the turn of the century the knowledge of the world has multiplied many times, doubling in the last five years. Our standard of living has multiplied as quickly, and we live in an affluent society surrounded by tremendous opportunities. From the development of penicillin we have now progressed to transplants. A computer can, in a couple of seconds, solve a mathematical problem that would require the efforts of hundreds of accountants working over a period of weeks or months.

While enjoying material wealth, we are plagued with a variety of physical ills that are psychological in origin. Young people have more and are satisfied less. Race riots, venereal disease, illegitimate births, narcotics addiction, divorce, suicide, and crime are merely overt symptoms of the distress and personal dissatisfaction that exist among people today. The rapid development of our technological world is matched by our society's social degeneration. Crime is rising faster than the population, with a major crime every 8½ seconds, three murders every 2 hours. Each year, thousands of children run away from home and nearly one out of three marriages ends in divorce. Why do we suffer such social stress and personal dissatisfaction while enjoying such material success?

Observe technological change. We see great breakthroughs in science, such as Einstein's theory of relativity. The result: on December 2, 1942, nuclear fission. Less than three years later, on July 16, 1945, near Alamogordo, New Mexico, the first atom bomb is exploded. In science great breakthroughs are applied and the results are almost immediate, but what about breakthroughs in human behavior and human relations? Here too we have had great breakthroughs, but why have they not been applied?

While the technological segment of our society is changing rapidly, a large part of our population is becoming obsolete through failure to keep pace. Women who were raised to take care of the home and children find that the new technological conveniences are giving them time to do whatever they would like to do. Yet all too often they become frustrated because they are not prepared for the opportunity to achieve on their own. Men who become proficient in a particular skill, whether blacksmithing at the turn of the century or engineering today, all too often find their skills obsolete. More than ever before, people must be able to change, to adapt, in order to capitalize on new opportunities rather than remain in the past and become obsolete. Yet why do people often have so much difficulty changing? What is stopping *you* from bridging the gap between where you are and where you really want to be?

To answer this question is the purpose of this book.

What characteristics do we find in successful people that are missing in most others? Why are some people able to adapt and capitalize on the opportunities offered by a changing society while others become obsolete? Do special qualities exist within the individual who becomes emotionally and financially self-sufficient?

You should find the following exercise worthwhile. Write on the lines below the factors you believe determine success:

_____

_____

_____

_____

_____

Desire

Traditionally, a burning desire to succeed has been considered a primary factor for success. The salesman who *has* this desire will overcome the irritations of selling and will succeed.

In the famous Battle of Marathon, the Greek soldier Pheidippides ran 25 miles, motivated by the desire to bring the news of victory. This desire numbed the pain and drove him beyond physical endurance; but once the goal was achieved, desire was no longer needed and Pheidippides collapsed and died. As long as you have a need to win, the desire will numb the frustration that comes with striving. How great is *your* desire to gain the material and emotional self-sufficiency that comes with continuous growth and achievement?

What experiences have you had that contributed to your determination to win? Have you identified with self-sufficient people who have inspired you to create your *own* independence—or with people who tend to be security-oriented? Why isn't your desire greater?

Yet doesn't everyone begin with a desire to do well financially, to achieve something that proves how good he is, to gain recognition and pride in himself? These, after all, are the reasons why you try to achieve financial and creative goals, and therefore you *do* begin with desire. Then why is the desire lost so quickly that a majority of people will reach a point in life where they stop trying and never try again?

Everybody has had dreams of achieving something significant and has had a desire to convert those dreams into reality. Nevertheless, for most people, when the time comes to try, the desire is missing. But why? *What quality do some people have within them that, regardless of discouragement and disappointment, makes them keep trying until they capitalize on their desire and convert their dreams into reality?*

Being Goal-oriented

Another important requisite for success is to be goal-oriented. If you have not set any goals, then you are not going anywhere; and if you have set vague and wandering goals, you are going places in a vague and wandering way. The more goal-oriented you are, the more you will be motivated to make those sacrifices today that will bring you tomorrow's objectives.

You are the captain of a ship that has been prepared to carry a great cargo of fruits and vegetables. Finally you are ready. You leave the harbor and move out to the open sea. Now you must determine your course, *but what if you haven't decided on a destination?* Then your ship lies in the salty sea under a burning sun and gradually the cargo begins to rot. If you do not have a goal, the potential within you will begin to wither and die for lack of direction.

Know where you want to be in the future and you will understand why it is so important to make sacrifices today. List your goals on the following lines and be as specific as possible. List them in their order of importance, along with the means of achieving them, in order to better assure success.

_____

_____

_____

_____

_____

Everyone, in some way, desires success, wants to be financially independent and to achieve something significant, gain recognition, be proud of himself, have peace of mind. If being goal-oriented is so important—and nearly everyone has these same basic goals—then why do most people seem to lose interest in their goals so quickly? What secret wellspring do some people tap that enables them, regardless of what might happen, to continue trying?

Knowledge

A third characteristic of success is knowledge. The more competent you become, the more confident you will be when faced with new situations and the greater will be your impact on others. You know you cannot be very confident in prospecting if you do not know what prospecting techniques to use. You know you cannot feel very enthusiastic in making a presentation if you do not know what to say. You know you cannot feel very aggressive when closing if you do not know any closing techniques. Knowledge is power.

Yet in many industries *the more competent the salesman becomes, the closer he comes to termination,* until, just as he knows what he is talking about, he quits! Now, why is this true with most people and why do others, regardless of what occurs, *capitalize* on their knowledge and *achieve* their goals?

If there is any doubt in your mind, watch the new salesman. The one characteristic he has on the first day on the job is a real desire to do well, and the one thing he lacks is knowledge. With this desire he makes a real effort, yet six months to a year later, just as he is becoming competent, he quits.

Confidence

This success characteristic adds strength to desire, builds a solid foundation for goal striving, and creates emotional competence. With confidence a man takes command of circumstances around and within him and drives through the obstacles of life. Yet nearly everyone attempts to achieve something of value in life, and they would not begin if they did not have some confidence they could succeed. Yet what ability is lacking in so many salesmen that they will lose their confidence so quickly? *What ingredient do we find in the successful salesman which, in spite of defeat, makes his confidence expand into consistent victories?*

Self-image

Finally, most people would contend that a major factor for success is having a good self-image. The successful salesman feels he is *worthy* of succeeding. Yet many people—like engineers, for example—have a good self-image and still have particular difficulty in selling. They have the college degree, often with graduate work. They are accustomed to a good salary, have a nice home, car, and family, and usually project competent, mature personalities. But they lack one ability, and thus too often are more concerned about protecting their self-image than succeeding. What, then, is this primary ability for success?

Simply this: *the ability to fail.* Most people are so afraid of failure and rejection that they spend their entire lives looking for comfortable situations where there are no risks or decisions to make and where they cannot possibly fail and be rejected. *Your ability to fail and continue trying will determine your success.* Without this ability all your goals will turn into empty dreams, your desire will be bottled up by fear, your confidence will be eroded by the first rejections, and all your knowledge and skills will be wasted for fear of failure.

We find that almost everyone beginning in sales, as in other fields, begins with a desire to succeed and a determination to be self-sufficient. When you consider the number who did *not* succeed you are left with one question: What happened to all that desire which, in a matter of weeks or months, was lost?

Desire Versus Doubts

As much as the salesman begins with a great deal of enthusiasm to succeed, he also begins with certain doubts that he might fail. He has had certain experiences in his past which indicate that he might fail in new and uncertain situations. He may remember Arthur Miller's *Death of a Salesman* and wonder if it is true. Then he might confront such comments from his parents as "I didn't send my son to college to become a salesman," or a friend might ask "Why would a nice guy like you want to become a salesman?" As though salesmen and nice people are two different types! While this may increase his doubts, he still has a great desire to make it on his own.

The first day on the job can be the next challenge to our enthusiastic salesman. As he begins his training he also gets to know his fellow salesmen, and invariably there are a couple of salesmen who are security-oriented and therefore negative. A discussion at lunch on the problems of the business can be very damaging. He is told about all the time that is lost with responsibilities such as meetings, paper work, servicing, people who forget appointments, as well as the discouragement of sales falling through, particularly when the commissions are already spent. All of a sudden the opportunities do not seem that bright, particularly when he is told that these problems will eliminate many new people in the first few months. Nevertheless, he still has considerable desire left.

Now it is his first day actually to sell and he gets on the telephone in an effort to line up an appointment. He calls thirty-seven people, and thirty-seven people say "I don't love you." Now those are not the exact words they use, but that is the way he reacts to them— and some of his doubts begin to develop into negative convictions. He wonders if he is really cut out to be a salesman.

In the classical pattern, he begins to avoid the rejection of cold prospecting and starts to become security-oriented in an effort to protect himself from further ego damage. He will sit at the office and send out direct mail, hoping that someone might send back a reply card. He finds himself spending hours with the same prospect, yet for some reason he is apprehensive about asking for the order and never does close.

Since he doesn't want to be rejected again, he grows more and more timid about approaching prospects. The next step is usually termination. The doubts have gradually converted into negative convictions, eroding the desire he originally had. Because he did not have the *ability to fail*, he *has* failed. And should another opportunity ever present itself, he will probably say, "No, I tried something like that before, and I failed. I am not about to try that again."

Experiments have shown that people become frustrated when they cannot make use of their abilities and potential. In fact, mental illness can develop when the *desire to grow* is frustrated by the *fear of failing* and the individual is mired in misery and defeat. Part of the frustration is removed if you are able to determine the cause of the fear. Why then do people have so much difficulty handling failure? To realize this, you must understand the nature of motivation.

What Really Motivates You?

If you understand your basic needs, you will understand what motivates you. Your needs are your motivators. They motivate you to set and achieve goals. People set goals only because their needs demand to be satisfied. Your needs generate within you your desire, which motivates you to achieve the goal. A goal, if it is realistic, is simply the extension of a need. Achieve the goal and you satisfy the need. By understanding your needs you will understand why you set certain goals and what motivates you. More important, it will dramatize why you may have so much difficulty with the threat of failure.

Make a list of what you believe are your six basic needs, beginning with the most important. To help you, imagine yourself on a desert island. What would you first be concerned about, what second, and so on?

Your Basic Needs: Survival and Security

Man's most basic need is survival; food, warmth (clothing and shelter), and companionship. A child deprived of human companionship cannot develop into a mature human being. We know that when infants are only fed and clothed but do not have human contact, they often become ill and die. The same is true with adults. In solitary confinement, an individual can easily lose his mind, with illness and death often following. Since you are already satisfying this need, we will not need to discuss it again.

Our second need is for security. In a primitive society this means protecting yourself from the local headhunters, while in our society it means protecting yourself from the local bill collectors. There you needed spears, here you need money.

Only a century ago, with a few necessities such as a rifle, a kettle, and a hatchet, a man could provide for himself and feel secure. He would make his own house, furniture, and clothing and obtain his own food. Today a person may have two cars, a color TV, a lovely home, and an excellent choice of foods and entertainment—as well as migraine headaches and ulcers.

A man went to a psychiatrist and said, "Doctor, I have a very serious problem."

"Well, what is your problem?"

"Doctor, I have a half-million dollar estate home in Beverly Hills. We take two vacations a year, one to Hawaii, the other to Europe. My son just turned sixteen and I bought him an Eldorado. Our children go to the finest private schools, we belong to a great country club, we have a beautiful yacht . . ."

At this point the psychiatrist blurted out, "Problem? *That's* a *problem?*"

"But Doctor, I make only $65 per week."

Now why is that humorous? Because it seems that no matter how well we do there is always an element of financial insecurity, thanks to the advertising industry which has done such a thorough job teaching us what we have to have in order to feel successful.

The Need To Achieve

Yet for all the emphasis on material wealth, we also know that in and of itself money has never assured happiness. All of us have known too many who have led empty lives pursuing symbols of success. It can be very depressing to believe that wealth will bring happiness, only to attain it and find no satisfaction. You need more. No matter what homage you pay to financial success, its greatest value is that it *creates the foundation you need to move into your next motivator, which is the need to achieve.*

Watch the successful salesman. Just as selling starts to become easy and he is making the kind of money he has always wanted, he asks to become a sales manager! So the manager explains to him why management is not the ideal position: "First of all, you have to take a pay cut; and there is a great deal more responsibility and pressure." You have probably heard of the Peter Principle, that "people rise to their level of incompetence." Nevertheless, the salesman still wants to try. This is because the growth-oriented salesman, as he begins to gain financial success, needs an even greater challenge. But the fact is that you do not have to be promoted to rise to your level of incompetence. You can do it right where you are, for if your present job becomes so easy as to lack challenge, your diminishing interest can cause incompetence.

Thus material success allows you to do whatever you want. What would you want to accomplish in life, if you could do whatever you *desired?* What you list will determine what achievement and success mean to you, whether a physical activity, a financial achievement, a family goal, comfort, or something of a personal interest, such as a hobby. At this point list the goals you would like to achieve.

_____

_____

_____

Need For Recognition

Why is it necessary to be strongly motivated to achieve? Because it is a means of satisfying your next need, which is the need for recognition. *The major reason most people will try to achieve something of importance is to gain approval from others.* What is more depressing and discouraging than to accomplish something worthwhile and not be appreciated? Without praise, achievement is all too often a meaningless and even frustrating experience—a hollow triumph.

The motivator can be referred to as the need for recognition, love, approval, praise, respect, or acceptance. The word varies, but only based on the role. The child seeks attention; the businessman, recognition; the young woman, love; the military leader, respect—it is all the same basic concept. This is the reason why, in a contest, salesmen will often work harder and make more money than they need in order to gain recognition.

Need For Identity

Yet recognition from others is only important when it satisfies your next need, and this is the need for identity. You may spend a major part of your life in a search for yourself, to discover who you are and what you can do. When someone tells you what a good job you have done, you gain recognition and a greater sense of your own worth. Result: the kind of positive self-image you must have.

Yet man still needs more. What of the film stars and other notables who committed suicide because they gained financial success but not happiness—achieved levels of accomplishment and recognition and still felt unsuccessful—and finally gained a sense of identity but not the inner satisfaction they so badly needed?

Need For Self-acceptance

All these needs must be satisfied, but only in order to satisfy your primary motivator. This is the need for self-acceptance. *Without self-acceptance there can be no personal satisfaction.* The more you like yourself the happier you will be, for success is the satisfaction of basic needs which culminate in self-acceptance. Tell me how much you accept or like yourself and you will tell me how successful you are.

Expectations

There is one important factor that influences how much an individual must succeed before he can accept himself, and that is his expectations. Each individual has different expectations which are primarily determined by the influence of others. As an example, Johnny grows up and his parents tell him, "We don't expect much of you. Remember Uncle Harry who died drunk in the street? And none of us has even finished high school. We have never done well, and we don't expect much of you either." Now what happens to Johnny when he does fail in life? He says "That was to be expected." And when he succeeds, "How did that happen? I must be lucky."

Then we have the child who is told by one parent, "If you don't put your nose to the grindstone, you will be a bum," and by the other parent, "I expect great things of you." These thoughts create both a negative challenge and high expectation which drive him to be successful, and if he ever slows down he becomes dissatisfied. If you do not know into which category you fit, here is a simple but effective way to find out: When you succeed, do you tend to level off and enjoy it for awhile, or are you so anxious for the next level that you often have difficulty enjoying what you have just attained? Of course, if you tend to level off and relax, it indicates that your expectations could be higher; but if you are so anxious that you often have difficulty enjoying the process of striving, then it indicates that you may be too demanding of yourself. You might achieve more if you were not so anxious.

What Demotivates You?

Now we reach a major question. If the primary need is to accept yourself, which is satisfied by discovering how good you are, which comes from acceptance by others, which is gained through achievement, then why do we find that *more than half our population spend their entire lives avoiding achievement?* The reason—*fear of failure.*

"Fear of failure" is only three words . . . but why do they have such a negative impact? You try to achieve in order to gain approval from others, but what happens when you try and fail? You get the opposite of what you were looking for—you get rejection. You are looking for approval because you want to discover how good you are; but if you are rejected, you discover instead that you are not as good as you would like to think you are. You are trying to find out what you can do so that you may accept yourself—but if you discover weaknesses instead, what then? Feelings of self-rejection.

Watch the child as he tries something new. He has a desire to achieve and gain attention that will help him feel important, yet he has certain doubts in his mind. Invariably, the greater the risk the greater the doubt. Every time he tries to achieve and fails, the doubts begin to turn into negative convictions that he should not have tried in the first place. Gradually he begins to develop an anxiety which motivates him to protect himself, and he falls victim of the common ailment—the inability to handle failure. Are adults any different?

We find that many people are willing to sacrifice the expansion of their own feelings of self-worth in order to avoid feelings of self-depreciation which result from having tried and failed. Most people depend on others for approval because of past conditioning—depending on parents, teachers, and friends for attention or acceptance. The challenge is to achieve your goals without worrying, en route to your success, about what people say. Very specifically, *you must find your acceptance within yourself and be self-sufficient.*

Needs Versus Fears

Many people feel the major causes of anxiety are arguments and conflict with others. Would you agree that the major causes are actually arguments and conflicts with yourself? There are five major arguments you can have with yourself based on the conflict between needs and antineeds. Review the following five conflicts in question form.

Which is more important to you?
1. To gain financial self-sufficiency or avoid financial insecurity
2. To achieve something significant or to avoid failure
3. To gain recognition or avoid rejection
4. To discover your strengths or avoid discovering weaknesses
5. To gain self-acceptance or to avoid ego damage

Everyone is motivated because we all have the same basic needs, as well as the same basic fears. Do you ever find yourself ready to get out of bed in the morning but instead go back to sleep? Do you ever begin a project your spouse asked you to do but for some reason stop halfway through? Do you ever find yourself looking forward to achieving a particular goal and yet avoiding it at the same time? You—all of us—are motivated and demotivated at the same time.

Success Patterns

Your ability to become successful depends on the degree of your self-acceptance. Your self-acceptance is based on success patterns, which require that you have the ability to fail and continue trying. There is a breaking point: each individual can handle only so much failure before he wants to quit. *The amount of acceptance you have of yourself relates directly to the amount of failure you can tolerate before you stop trying and thus stop achieving.*

In this respect, life is similar to a poker game. The way you win chips at poker is to gamble by moving them out onto the table and taking a chance. If you lose too often you may take what you have left and cash them in. You begin each day in a similar way. You extend yourself emotionally by getting your ego involved, and if you win you feel more expansive and become more aggressive about trying. If you begin to lose, you may find yourself protecting what you have left and withdrawing. Often you may have an argument with your wife in the morning, and by the time you leave you cannot handle any more ego damage for the rest of the day.

Ask yourself: "Are there responsibilities I am avoiding, thus reducing my chance for success? Are there certain kinds of people I am reluctant to get involved with? How much failure can I handle before I want to quit? How many calls can I make before I need to rest, and am I making enough calls to succeed financially?" The desire to be successful is of little value if you cannot handle the necessary failure en route to that success. If your failure level determines your success, then how has it developed?

The problem with most people is that they are not prepared for risk situations. They have been protected from failure, which is part of life's greatest challenges. As an example, in school we have to get nine out of ten right for an A, eight for a B, seven for a C, six for a D, and with only five right we are in very serious trouble. Yet in industrial research and development, a company has about five successful products for every hundred serious ideas that are initially investigated. But most salesmen wouldn't dream of telling their manager, "I've just failed ninety-five times out of a hundred. I'm a big success." How does this apply to you? *Can you make a hundred calls in a day based on fifteen per hour and come back enthusiastic because you succeeded five times out of a hundred?*

People are conditioned not only by school experiences but also by their parents: Be popular, be accepted, fit in, be nice, adjust. But the real challenge is to determine the best way to take *command* rather than deferring to the easiest alternative and seeking protection.

While most people have never been prepared for risk situations, some have had bad experiences but came back and tried again. Others fail and stop trying. Can you remember a time in childhood when you wanted to participate in something important, maybe a sporting event or a school play? You built up your ego the way you would inflate a balloon. Finally the day came and you were ready to face it, only to have someone stick a pin in that balloon. And that was the end of your effort. The next time you began to dream of what you wished to do, you thought back to the past failure experience and, rather than risk defeat again, you continued dreaming. Gradually, for lack of effort, you even stopped dreaming. You need to have not only the ability to *dream* of succeeding but also the ability to *fail* while in the process of converting your dreams into reality.

For most of us, ego damage is the result of minor occurrences. The problem of public speaking, for example, is a serious one for most individuals. As children, if we made an error while giving a speech in class, our fellow students might laugh. Since it was an unfamiliar situation to begin with, we may have had some doubts about doing it in the first place. The failure caused disapproval or ridicule which, in turn, caused the doubts to develop into negative beliefs. We may then have established certain negative habits intended to protect us from similar situations and future failures. Unfortunately these negative habits also prevent us from succeeding.

It is important to be honest with yourself, to understand why you play certain "games," and why you are avoiding the risk of ego damage. First, you should list all those challenges in life you feel are threatening, things you would like to do but have problems doing. Then you should try to determine which particular experiences you may have had that would cause you to feel that way. If the desire for achievement is checkmated by fear of failure, you will be blocked from reaching your goals; but even more frustrating is not knowing what is causing the problem. Once you understand the nature of these fears, you can establish the action to be taken in removing them.

Make a list of those experiences you find threatening, such as selling a new product, prospecting, overcoming objections, closing, or asking for referrals. Then determine what you believe to be the cause of these fears.

Past experiences	Threatening situations	Solution

II

Attitudes toward Failure

We have discussed the fact that you gain self-acceptance through success patterns. Now we come to a transitional question. How can you step into new situations in which you have never succeeded before and yet feel confident of succeeding? Each individual has the same fears of failure, rejection, and ego damage; yet the successful individual has an ability that allows him to step into threatening situations with confidence and self-assurance. He either *disengages* these fears or *constructively channels them into a force for achievement*. How do you react to your fears of failure, regardless of what level of success you may presently be experiencing?

_____

_____

_____

_____

_____

Your First Solution

The successful individual disengages these fears of failure by having a different attitude toward failure. He never sees failure as failure but only as. . . . How would you finish that statement?

_____

_____

_____

_____

_____

_____

_____

Learning Process

The first positive attitude toward failure is that there is no such thing as failure but only a learning process. As an example, Thomas Edison had invented the light bulb but could not find a filament that would work. The filament would last a few seconds or at best a few minutes. One day he was asked, "Mr. Edison, you have tried a thousand times and you have failed a thousand times, are you discouraged?" Edison replied, "No, I am not discouraged because I have not failed a thousand times, I have only found a thousand different ways that it doesn't work." And with that attitude toward failure, we have the light bulb today.

Edison had the ability to fail and to continue trying because each failure to him was a learning process which told him why the filament had lasted as long as it had.

Now, how can you apply this attitude to selling? As an example, when do you have a chance to try new prospecting or closing techniques? Imagine that you have a prospect who is a friend, and you know you have just what he needs and are ready to close. Would you try some new closing technique you have never used before? Not likely. So when *do* you have an opportunity to try something new—except when everything is failing and there appears to be nothing to lose?

A life insurance salesman has just closed ten times without success, and in a final effort asks the prospect to sign a letter which is written to the salesman himself:

Dear Jack:

I have listened to you close ten times and I have firmly decided that I shall never buy any additional life insurance.

Sincerely,

The prospect turns to the salesman and says, "I'll sign your letter, but this is no testimonial for you. Who would you want to show a letter like that to?" "I am going to show it to your wife after you die." Now, I am not recommending a technique like this, but the salesman *did* have nothing to lose and *did* try a new idea.

You can *expect* to confront failure and rejection no matter what your objectives may be. But how do you react when your efforts are fruitless and comments from others are negative? Are you afraid of rejection? How much of it can you take before you want to quit? What happens if someone criticizes you? Do you take it personally? Whenever you see a lack of success as failure or criticism as rejection, your fears of failure and rejection will be triggered. Once these demotivators are activated, they begin to generate anxiety, and the anxiety motivates you to stop, quit, terminate, withdraw, or avoid.

If, instead, you view failure as *an opportunity to try new ideas,* you will trigger the positive needs to achieve and to prove how good you are. These needs will generate within you a desire to continue striving, and thus you will make a second effort. For these reasons you should accept your responsibility to yourself by realizing that *you* decide whether you avoid or try again because *you* are the one who decides whether you are experiencing emotions of enthusiasm or anxiety. This is because you are the one who decides which needs are being triggered—needs to avoid failure or needs to achieve something significant. Whether they be positive or negative is determined by your attitude toward failure, approaching it as failure or as an opportunity to develop new ideas. You are the one who decides what your attitude will be toward the same negative experiences that everyone else confronts.

	Attitude	Motivator	Emotion	Behavior	Results
Failure, Criticism, or a Risk Situation	As a threat to your ego	To avoid Failure and Rejection	Frustration and Anxiety	Avoid and Retreat	**Negative**
	As an Opportunity to try new ideas	To achieve and gain Self-esteem	Desire and Enthusiasm	Continue Trying	**Positive**

From this day forward, whenever you fail, you should ask yourself first, "Why did I last as long as I did?" Most people will ask, "What did I do wrong?" While that might be academically correct, it invariably triggers doubts in their minds. Whenever you fail and ponder what you did wrong, you tend to convert these doubts into negative convictions which motivate you to avoid such situations again.

It is like the child who has just received a bad report card. As he goes to his·father to have the report card signed, he thinks, "Maybe the reason I am doing so poorly is because I have poor study habits. I think I am lazy, and maybe I really don't care about school. Then maybe it might be because I am not that smart." He shows the report card to his father, who becomes very angry. Finally he turns to his son and, with extreme irritation, tells him, "The problem with you is that you don't care about school, you have rotten study habits, and you are lazy as well as stupid." As the child leaves the room he no longer has any doubts in his mind. Now he knows for sure why he can't do it. From this day forward, if he fails, he will feel it is understandable; and if he succeeds, he will feel he is lucky.

We have a tendency to do the same thing to ourselves by being too aware of *why we fail* and not aware enough of *why we succeed.* Again, from this day forward, whenever you fail, ask yourself, "What did I do to last as long as I did?" Then you can ask yourself, "What could I have done to last longer?"

As an example, when the insurance salesman calls on a prospect and introduces himself, he finds that the mere mention of insurance draws a negative response.

"Hello, my name is John Smith and I would like to talk to you about insurance."

"No, I have all I need."

For most people a no is synonymous with rejection, and they try to avoid the same response again. For the salesman, this means discontinuing the conversation. The salesman who approaches it as a learning process will ask himself why he succeeded, because *he has lasted five seconds.* He will realize that it was because he picked up the telephone and actually tried. Seeing this as success, he will now try to see if he can keep the light burning a few seconds longer.

"Hello, my name is John Smith and I would like to speak to you about your life insurance." Getting the same response ("No, I have all I need"), the salesman then asks, "Good, how much do you have?"

"Ten thousand dollars' worth."

Rather than seeing this as failure, the salesman asks himself why he has lasted *twice* as long and realizes it was because he has tried a second time by asking a question.

Let's try it once more: "Hello, my name is John Smith, and I would like to talk to you about your life insurance."

"No, I have all I need."

"Good, how much do you have?"

"Ten thousand dollars' worth."

"Well, I guess you don't plan on being dead very long." Again I would not necessarily recommend it. Nevertheless, you will learn something from each approach you try. Gradually you will develop a repertoire of techniques which will help you in almost any situation. It all begins with a new attitude of seeing each rejection not as a rejection but as an opportunity to try new ideas.

Investment

The second attitude toward failure is to look at it as an investment. As a salesman you probably do not make any investment in the company. You do not invest in the office, the telephone, advertising, or the secretary. Yet you make the most difficult investment of all. You invest your ego in the business. If you are a residential real estate salesman you will make one hundred cold calls and you will get three appointments, from which you will gain two listings and one house will sell. The result—about $400 in your pocket. Yet with this guaranteed formula for success the salesman will do this only a couple of times, succeed a couple of times, and never do it again. The reason is that the $400 at the end in no way compensated for the ninety-nine rejections en route to that $400. For this reason your success does not come so much from the sale as from your ability to handle the failure en route to that sale. Therefore you should determine the value of each failure experience you must go through in order to succeed. *Divide the number of negatives you confront each week into your average weekly income and you will discover how much you are being paid whenever you are turned down.* In the real estate example it will be $4 per no, and this is a rather conservative estimate.

From this day on, whenever a prospect is hostile to you, I would like you to say, "Thank you for the $4" (or whatever you have determined to be the amount of money that you make per no). Often the prospect will ask, "What do you mean by the $4?" This gives you the opportunity to tell him, "Most people are rather rude to me, as you have been, but you at least speed me on to the individual who will be receptive to some new ideas, and that is where I gain my income. The reason why I do so well is that individuals like you help me to reach receptive people more quickly."

There are several benefits to be gained by using this technique. First, many aggressive people turn hostile when somebody tries to sell them something. Yet if the salesman reacts aggressively, they respect him, and suddenly the salesman gains a positive reaction. Most prospects, on the other hand, are passive personalities who frequently become frustrated because they cannot control the situation. They may take out their frustration on people they cannot see, such as you when you call them. When you react back with empathy, you embarrass them—as they should be embarrassed—and you may also gain a positive response from them. Equally important, each time you use this technique you will reinforce the basic truth that there is no such thing as failure but only opportunities for making money, *for you are paid every time someone turns you down!*

Law of Averages

The third attitude that disengages the "antineeds" is to approach risk situations as a game or to play the law of averages. You need to study failure and rejection objectively, as a statistical experience rather than an emotional one that will cause anxiety. As an example, the IBM computer salesman is conditioned to success. He has the degrees, he is hired by a company which is very selective and pays him well for a lengthy training period, he sells for a company that has an extremely good image and controls 70 percent of the data processing equipment market—with more than twenty other major companies sharing the other 30 percent—and he must score well on the IBM IQ tests in order to be accepted.

All of a sudden he may find himself in a down market where he is no longer getting the same kind of acceptance as before. People might be canceling orders for his equipment, which he is not used to, and price may be more of a factor than it was previously. He is hassled by his boss about quota and by his wife about buying the new house he promised. He is used to looking at his world as a flow chart and analyzing things statistically, but where do you place ego damage and depression in a flow chart? He has difficulty approaching anxiety, rejection, and failure in the same analytical way that he views the rest of his life. If he could approach failure statistically and analyze rejection objectively, he would disengage the negative emotions and the fears of failure, thus neutralizing the problem.

In approaching failure statistically or as a game, you give yourself a point every time you call on someone who is not in, two points if he is in but does not want to speak to you, five points if he speaks to you and then stands you up and does not even give you the courtesy of telling you he has canceled the appointment. You score twenty points if he allows you to give a presentation and then decides to buy from your competitor instead, fifty points if he buys your product and then cancels afterwards, and seventy-five points if he cancels after you have been paid and spent the commissions. How many points can you score in a day?

How many times will you usually fail before you can expect to succeed? How many times did Babe Ruth strike out on his way to 714 home runs? He struck out 1,330 times, but to Babe Ruth it was all part of the process of succeeding. In fact, Babe Ruth, when he struck out, often swung so hard that he would fall in the dirt. As he walked back to the dugout, having struck out, covered with dirt, and the fans booing, he would take his hat off to the fans; and when he hit a home run, as he went back to the dugout, he would take off his hat to the fans. To him *failure and success were all part of the same process of achieving*, and one could not be gained without experiencing the other.

You've probably heard of Ty Cobb and his great ability to steal bases. In 1911 he stole 96 bases, but have you ever heard of Max Carey? In 1922, Carey stole 51 bases out of 53 tries for a 96 percent success ratio, compared with Cobb's 70 percent based on 96 out of 134 attempts. Carey was careful not to fail and hardly ever did, but you remember Cobb because he succeeded so many more times. You must come to realize that *people are not remembered by how few times they fail but by how often they succeed*. Are you so concerned about succeeding that you cannot handle failure and thus do not gain the success you deserve?

Negative Feedback

A fourth positive attitude toward failure is to approach it as the negative feedback you *need* in order to make changes in your course of direction.

In selling, you have to welcome objections, for the only way you can overcome them is to determine what they are. The sooner you recognize them, the sooner you can resolve them. As an example, why is a torpedo always zigzagging? It is getting feedback from its target that tells it it is off course. However, it has the ability to make course corrections in order to stay on target. Now what would happen if a torpedo had an ego and every time it received negative feedback it took it personally?

It could take one of five incorrect actions. It could give up and go to the bottom, which would make it like some salesmen who, when they decide to quit, never show up for their last paycheck. It could blow up, as do some people who, because of their inability to handle failure and rejection, commit suicide. It could just float in the ocean until someone came by and helped it out. It could turn around and go home, which is disastrous—and a person who cannot handle rejection in the field will usually confront more rejection from the office or home when he has not succeeded. In fact, if you will think more about *tomorrow's* rejection from your boss or spouse than about *today's* objection from the prospect, you won't be bothered as much. Finally, the torpedo could develop an "I don't give a damn" attitude, disregard the feedback, and just keep on going, lost forever on the endless sea.

Actually, man is very similar to the torpedo. He is a goal-seeking mechanism that spends a major part of his day striving to achieve specific objectives. Man has a sensing device that picks up feedback which tells him when he is off target, and he has the ability to make changes in his course in order to stay on target. But man's sensing device tends to be oversensitive. Therefore, when he receives negative feedback, he all too often takes it personally and goes off course.

If the individual sees failure as the negative feedback he needs in order to make changes in his course, then, when he fails, he has the ability to say, "This is very interesting. I wonder why I am being rejected? Did I say something wrong or maybe come on too strong? Perhaps I haven't determined how the individual feels and therefore he feels I cannot really relate to him. Then again, maybe he is just hostile and taking it out on me. It could be that he has had a bad experience." Again, your ability to change your attitude toward failure has a dramatic impact on how you handle the same negative situations everyone else confronts in life. If you take the negative feedback as the information you need in order to make corrections in your course, you will capitalize on failure, welcome criticism, and stay on target.

Responsibility

The fifth attitude toward failure is to realize that if you have fulfilled your responsibility to your customer as best you can, then you should not take failure and rejection personally. One of the stockbroker's major fears is that someone will lose money on his recommendations and therefore reject him. Yet if he originally explained to the prospect the benefits *and* the risks and supplied him with an alternative "buy" recommendation so he had a choice, then when the prospect makes his decision it is *his* responsibility as well. The stockbroker has fulfilled his obligation, regardless of the outcome, by having done the best he possibly could. If you apply all your thoughts and energies to any effort, then you have fulfilled your responsibility and should compliment yourself on your courage rather than criticize yourself each time you might fail.

If you have discovered a prospect's inner need, you have the responsibility to do everything within your ability to motivate him to action. If you have done the best you can to help solve his problem and he will not agree, you cannot feel rejected. At the same time if, for fear of being rejected, you do not fulfill your responsibility, then you should reject yourself.

Humor

Your sixth positive attitude toward risk situations is to approach them with a sense of humor. You know that you are not very effective when you approach a new or difficult situation with the fear that you might fail. But haven't there been times when you *have* failed and later were able to laugh about it and tell someone of your difficult or embarrassing experience? Laugh earlier. The sooner you can laugh about something, the sooner you can react positively and again be effective.

The next time you have a discouraging day, remember the astronaut, suited up and heading for the rocket ship, who was stopped by a reporter and asked, "When you get up into orbit, what would happen if your rockets don't fire and you can't get back down?" He replied, "It's going to spoil my day." If you can approach the risk situations of life with a sense of humor, then your success is guaranteed. In fact, after the astronaut had landed, the Senate had a hearing to ask him questions about his flight. One senator asked him, "What were you thinking about as you were coming back through reentry?" and he replied, "I was thinking that this capsule I was in was manufactured by the lowest bidder." If you can develop this positive attitude toward the challenges in your life, you will trigger positive needs instead of fears, determination instead of anxiety, motivation to strive rather than the wish to avoid.

Opportunities for Growth

Our seventh and last constructive attitude toward failure is to approach difficult situations as opportunities for growth. Steel is tempered not by baking under the sun but by being subjected to the white heat of the furnace. Similarly, you cannot temper the strength of your inner self except by plunging into the intensities of life's experiences. Selling can be a grand adventure or a painful experience, depending on your attitude. If you become security-oriented and seek ways of protecting yourself from failure, you will also be sacrificing success. The recommendation is to be *growth-oriented,* to be *self-sufficient,* and to *find your acceptance within yourself.*

One of the writer's favorite cartoons is of Andy Capp, stretched out on the couch in his usual sleeping position. His wife walks by and exclaims, "You know, you are nothing but a failure." With that he leaps up and yells, "I am not a failure. How can you call me a failure? Why, I've never tried." And that is the way each of us is in certain areas of our life. You have heard it said: "Better to have tried and failed than never to have tried at all," but I find too often that people behave as though it is better not to try. That way they can tell themselves that if they had tried, they would have succeeded. That way they take no chances. Is it possible that there are abilities within you that you have never tried to use because you did not want to fail? If so, you *have* failed in that situation for lack of ever trying.

If you recognize that your success in life is based on your ability to fail and continue trying, then you must make a decision—a decision to change your attitude toward failure. You must see it as a learning process and as an investment. You must approach it as a game and realize it is the negative feedback you need in order to change your course. You must realize that if you fulfill your responsibility, then you cannot take failure personally, because you have done the best you possibly could. You must approach a risk situation with a sense of humor and as an opportunity for growth and achievement. The basic contention is that if the more you fail the more you succeed, then it cannot be failure *but only part of the process of succeeding*.

A quotation which is worth memorizing is by a man who never was afraid to fail, Theodore Roosevelt: "Far better it is to dare mighty things, to win glorious triumphs, even though checkered with failure, than to take rank with those poor spirits who neither enjoy much nor suffer much because they live in the grey twilight that knows neither victory nor defeat."

III

Anxiety and Creative Energy

Imagine a salesman who has a great desire to succeed but is also afraid to fail. Because of his desire to succeed he is continually trying, but because of his fear of failure he is continually experiencing frustration. Psychological frustration triggers anxiety, which results in depression. Each individual has an anxiety level which has two parts, comfort zone and danger zone. Each individual can handle only so much depression before he begins to reach the danger zone of his anxiety level, causing him to terminate at that point in order to avoid further anxiety. Or, rather than quit, he may become marginal in an effort to continue operating without reaching his danger zone. Most people tend to be the depressed type, bottling up anxiety until it motivates them to withdraw. The danger in becoming depressed is that it is self-destructive. It neutralizes energy and creativity and causes such physiological problems as ulcers, hypertension, and migraine headaches. How do you feel when you are depressed? What impact does depression have on your effectiveness and on your relations with others?

Then we have some people who do not believe in quitting or becoming marginal. They boast that they don't *get* ulcers, they *give* them. Rather than bottling up the anxiety in the form of depression, they get it out of their systems by turning it on others. Hostility is good in the sense that the anxiety is eliminated. Nevertheless, the negative impact on others usually leads to negative results which can create vicious cycles, culminating in ineffectiveness and internal dissatisfaction. Do you tend to be the hostile type?

			Anxiety Level
Goals blocked by obstacles →	Frustration triggers anxiety →		Danger Zone
Anxiety results in depression →	Triggers hostility →	May lead to release of creative energy →	Comfort Zone

Finally, anxiety can be eliminated in the form of creative energy. Successful people can often be just as frustrated as those who fail, but they will have conditioned themselves to burn it out of their systems in such a way that they become more effective. In fact, some of our most successful people have the greatest doubts or feelings of inadequacy. What could be the relationship between fears and success? If the individual's fears are not that great then his anxiety is not that great, and thus smoking, drinking, watching television, or sleeping late may resolve that anxiety. Yet if the feelings of inadequacy become very strong, they may create so much anxiety that traditional methods of resolving anxiety do not relieve the pressure. If the individual becomes hostile, it only creates negative reactions in others, which, in turn, increase his own internal anxiety. Gradually he is forced to develop methods that will eliminate the anxiety while helping him to achieve levels of success, thus resolving the inner doubts as well as the anxiety. For these reasons it is crucial that you learn to say to yourself "I enjoy converting anxiety into creative energy."

Depressed, Hostile, or Creative

Now, what type of individual do you tend to be, the depressed type, the hostile type, or the creative type? Actually, most people are all three. The question, rather, is why do you stay depressed as long as you do, what causes you to become hostile, and what causes you to become creative? As an example, we can take the hypothetical case of a sales manager who ordinarily wakes up in the morning at a very calm level. We can say that the danger zone begins at 700, the break point is 1,000, and this particular sales manager wakes up in the morning at a very calm 50.

This particular morning, as he reads the stock market report, he discovers that his stock has just dropped two more points. Since he is a very calm type of individual this causes him only the mildest of anxiety, and he is now at 150. At the breakfast table his wife reads the same stock market report and sees fit to express her views on his ability as an investor. He is now at 300. He has to give a sales meeting this morning to kick off the new month, and by the time he gets out of the house he is late for work. Fighting the rush hour traffic brings him to 400.

Before he starts his sales meeting, he checks the mail to find that the newly arrived production figures tell him that his office is the lowest in the region. Now he is at 500, but before he goes into the sales meeting the phone rings and his boss tells him, "It is your fault that your office is the lowest in the region. Now the monkey is on your back, and if you can't do the job we'll get someone who can." He walks into that meeting jumping up and down at 700 and has twelve salesmen sitting there at a calm 50. He then goes on to tell them, "The office is the lowest office in the region because of your failure. The monkey is on my back, and it's on your back as well. If I go I am going to take half of you with me." When he walks out of there he is at a calm 50, and twelve salesmen walk out of the meeting jumping up and down at 700.

A few days later he wonders why they are all sitting there doing nothing. He begins to realize that maybe he came on a little too strong with them and at that particular point he discusses with each of them individually what their problems might be, tailoring ideas to their particular needs, and in some cases going out into the field with them to get them started again. He becomes creative. He stayed depressed as long as it was not that serious or he was in a role in which he couldn't take it out on another individual. He became hostile to the point where he could not handle it any longer, and angry with those over whom he had authority. He became creative when he cooled off enough to be objective and realized that it was not working for his benefit—and you are the same way. What will you start doing today that will take you out of depression and hostility more quickly and bring you into a creative process of achieving?

Still, there are some people who are very depressed types and have considerable difficulty becoming creative. They are afraid that if they try to use their anxiety creatively they may project aggressiveness and threaten people and thus be rejected in return. For this reason they never express their anxiety or put it to creative use. The result: Peaks and valleys of success rather than consistent success, a negative impact on others because of a general withdrawal and moodiness, and finally personal dissatisfaction. Strange as this may sound, it is necessary for this type of individual actually to learn how to become hostile. It is not that we recommend hostility, but you cannot be so afraid of being irritable that you are unable to express your anxiety outwardly in the form of creative energy.

Anxiety-eliminating Techniques

With these thoughts in mind, what techniques are you presently using to eliminate anxiety? You may think you experience considerable rejection, and thus anxiety, in your business, but is it as great as what a stockbroker experiences in a down market? How would you feel if your friends called you and said, "Jack, what have I ever done to you that you would want to do this to me?" or if your relatives called you and said, "Jack, what have I ever done to you that I should deserve this?" How would you feel if your mother called you and said, "Son, my pension. Why have you done this to me?" Now that is *real* rejection, and it will cause considerable anxiety. The stockbroker starts early in the morning with phone calls, research, and rejection, and by five o'clock he realizes he is just too uptight to walk into the house right away. The kids should not see him in the condition he is in at the moment. How does the stockbroker traditionally eliminate anxiety?

He stops off in a cocktail lounge and has a double martini, and the drink does eliminate the anxiety of the day; but as he sits there drinking, he begins to think of the rush-hour traffic. The only answer now is a second double martini. It helps for a while, but then he realizes what his wife is going to say to him at eight o'clock that night, when he comes in late, and she goes on about how "You don't care about me, slaving over the stove all day long and talking baby talk to your children all day while you are out in the world with your glamorous life." Well, he has had too much rejection all day long to have any more at this point.

Another double martini.

As he sits there drinking the third, he begins to realize he has wasted a whole night in a cocktail lounge. This bothers him so much that the only answer is a fourth double, and now there is only one last thought he could possibly have, and that is how he is going to feel the next morning when he wakes up. This bothers him so much that the only answer now is a fifth double. Then he is so relaxed there are no more thoughts, and therefore there is no more anxiety; but has he really solved his problems? Has the anxiety been converted into some form of achievement which will stop additional anxiety?

You need to develop techniques that eliminate anxiety and also convert the anxiety into creative energy. In this way you gain a sense of achievement which inhibits further anxiety. Examine, for this reason, the four major areas of your life: physical, business, family, and personal. You need to develop a technique of eliminating anxiety that will also give you a sense of achievement in each one of these four areas. For example, jogging a mile a day when you are irritated in order to achieve better physical condition; team prospecting when you feel depressed as a means of becoming more financially successful; spending more creative time with the family when experiencing stress. You should also have a few anxiety-relieving activities that are just plain fun. These might include sculpturing, reading, or taking a class in something you particularly enjoy. Each of these techniques allows you to work off your anxiety and at the same time gives you a sense of accomplishment and personal satisfaction.

Nevertheless, you will be more effective if you can eliminate the anxiety at the roots rather than at the surface. Resolve the causes of the anxiety and you will tend to operate more from a healthy desire to succeed than from the anxiety which comes from inner fears. For this reason you should understand the three major causes of anxiety and how to resolve these problems at the roots.

Expectations Versus Reality

The first cause of anxiety is based on a concept referred to as "expectations versus reality." The problem with most people is that they feel successful only when they succeed *most* of the time. Yet the salesman has to condition himself to the fact that he has to feel successful when he is *failing* most of the time.

In each of your responsibilities there is a ratio of success to failure. You must make a certain number of calls to gain an appointment and a certain number of presentations to make a sale, and that is reality. Now what are your expectations? Are they consistent with reality, or do you expect more than is realistic?

If you expect more than is realistic, you will become frustrated when you do not gain the success that you expect. This frustration creates anxiety, resulting in depression, hostility, or—one hopes—creative energy. Why do people, particularly salesmen, consistently experience this difficulty? Think back and recall what your success ratio was when taking tests or in interpersonal relations. As an example, in taking a test you may have expected to get eighty-five right out of one hundred, but how do you feel when you call on people and get negative responses most of the time? Most salesmen will feel that they have failed. To avoid this you have to tune your expectations into reality and realize that this is normal.

Recently a real estate salesman told me of driving out for an appointment to discuss listing a home, and as he arrived (on time) at eight o'clock, the lights suddenly went out. He thought, "That's kind of funny." He knocked on the door but no one answered. He knew they were in there so he knocked louder, but still no one answered. At this point he became irritated and proceeded to knock as hard as he could. Finally he heard the back door open up, a German shepherd came running around the side, and he got into his car just in time. Now did he take it personally? Did he feel rejected? If you work with homeowners and you have not had this experience yet, you have not made enough calls.

Oversensitivity

Remember the Peter Principle: "People rise to their level of incompetence." The primary reason is because of the conflict between expectations and reality. If a salesman can handle failure at one level, he will succeed and often be promoted into management; but at the management level the failure experiences become more intense. If he cannot handle the failure, he'll become defensive, and this usually leads to incompetence. He will have risen to his level. At the same time you should realize that you do not have to be promoted in order to rise to your level of incompetence. You can do it all in the same job. This is because, as you go from one aspect of your job into another, often you will find that you are becoming more emotionally involved, and failure will mean more ego damage.

If you were to send out direct mail and people did not respond, would that bother you? Probably not, because you are not emotionally involved; but what if you went door-to-door and someone slammed the door in your face? Now that might really bother you. You might become even more upset if someone bought from you and then canceled, but how would you feel if your spouse had gone out for a peanut butter sandwich two weeks ago and was not home yet? The challenge is that each success prepares you for the next level of success, but at each new level the emotional involvement becomes greater, thus making the intensity of possible failure greater. This causes you to become more sensitive to what might occur. At the point at which you become oversensitive you will find yourself becoming indecisive or defensive, cutting you off from your strengths and reducing your effectiveness.

Because of the importance of this concept you must again review all your responsibilities and, through discussion with others, determine the success-failure ratio in each responsibility. As an example, how many calls do you expect to make before getting an appointment? If you can gain only 10 percent and yet through self-evaluation you find that you expect 25 percent, you have a serious gap. This is the major reason why salesmen do not prospect. When they get five straight negative responses, they would rather not go any further. They expect a yes almost every time and—while it may come on the tenth try—they cannot go that far because their expectations are so out of line with reality that the resulting anxiety causes them either to avoid or overreact and thus to fail. You need to tune your expectations into reality.

YOUR EXPECTATIONS (Are They Realistic?)

Responsibility	What I Expect	What is Realistic	Necessary Solutions
Example:			Get referral where ratio of success is
Prospecting	1 appt. out of 5 calls	1 appt. out of 10 calls	more frequent

Conflict

The second major cause of frustration and anxiety is conflict. Each time you find yourself with more than one goal at one time and cannot achieve both, you will begin to experience psychological frustration, which triggers anxiety and leads to depression or hostility. In order to resolve the conflict at the root you need to know what is causing it.

The major conflict that people can experience begins with their primary need—to gain self-acceptance. This need motivates you to set and achieve goals. Conflicting with this positive need for self-acceptance is the antineed, which is the need to avoid losing self-acceptance or having your ego damaged. This antineed motivates people literally to set goals *not* to achieve. As an example, have you ever found yourself to be lazy, disorganized, or procrastinating? You may feel these are your problems, but actually they are *not* your problems. They are what you do to *protect* yourself from your problems; for as long as you are lazy you will never have time to do those things you are afraid to do, as long as you are disorganized you will never have a chance to work in those areas where you feel inadequate, and as long as you are procrastinating you will never have time to follow up on those prospects who, you are afraid, are not really prospects after all.

Laziness, disorganization, and procrastination are basically non-achieving goals that protect your ego from damage by cutting you off from trying and failing. Yet you cannot do both at the same time. You cannot achieve and avoid all at once. You cannot expand and defend, produce and protect all at the same time. Before discussing the final solutions for resolving conflict at the root, you should determine if there are any conflicts that you might be experiencing at this time.

Conflict can develop when others set goals for you, as when your family wants you home at night and your company wants you at a special training program at the same time. Often your goals conflict with those of others, as when your customer asks to see you just when you want to watch a sporting event. Usually it is a conflict between you and yourself, based on motivating needs and demotivating antineeds. At this point you should outline, on paper, the major conflicts that are causing frustration and anxiety for you at this time. Notice how often you experience each conflict as well as how frustrating each experience is. Then determine which conflicts should be resolved first, and follow the next five methods for conflict resolution.

List Your Conflicts

_____

_____

_____

_____

Quality Time

The first method is keynoted by quality time. If you really make full use of your potential and the time you *do* have, then you can often eliminate the conflict by achieving both goals at basically the same time. As an example, if you have a conflict between your family who want you home on a particular night and your manager who wants you to prospect, you may have no choice but to prospect. You might become upset and find yourself halfway to your danger zone. Now if you confront a few rejections on your first prospecting calls, you may start experiencing anxiety which motivates you to begin avoiding; so you start drinking coffee, sending out some direct mail, reviewing some training material, and making a few halfhearted prospecting calls. By the time the evening ends, you realize you have wasted your time and you might just as well have had gone home initially and achieved your family goal rather than working and achieving neither goal.

What if you had made full use of your potential? You could have started your calls earlier, and by moving quickly and effectively you could have completed the calls in at least two hours and still gotten home early enough to spend some quality time with your family rather than just watching television. Making full use of your potential can often resolve conflict at the roots, quickly and comfortably.

Why do many people make so little use of their potential? Because most of them are not aware of their strengths and abilities. In addition, they are too often conditioned to respond to their negative emotions rather than consciously controlling the process and resolving it at the roots. You know that you are not very effective when you are uptight about having more than you can handle. The stress, however, only reduces your effectiveness. You need to make full use of your ability, and often you will find that you can accomplish virtually everything in a reasonable period of time. Decide now which conflict can best be resolved by the greater use of your potential, and take action.

Communicate

If making full use of your potential is not the solution, then the second method is to communicate. Very often our anxiety originates from conflicts with others when they ask us to do something that conflicts with our personal goals or when they do not understand why our objectives are different from theirs. As an example, your manager may tell you how you should close and you may find yourself becoming irritable because you cannot see yourself saying it the way he suggests. Rather than allowing this conflict to frustrate you, how would you communicate to him? You might, for example, say, "Boss, your closing technique is just what I should be using, but I have difficulty fitting it to my personality. Could you spend a few minutes helping me change it to my style?"

Regardless of whether the conflict is between you and your customer, your business associates, or your family, you have to become more effective at communicating. Remember, the more involved you become, the more you need to communicate with others. Unfortunately, most people react emotionally to conflict, rather than consciously determining the cause and controlling the situation.

Why do people have so much difficulty communicating? We have already discussed the first reason, that in your effort to resolve a problem you might only make it worse and thus experience more failure and rejection. Another reason is that you *may not yet have communicated to yourself*. How can you expect to communicate to others if you have not first decided what the problem is? Too often we excuse our ill humor with a remark like "I guess I woke up on the wrong side of the bed." From this point on, whenever you find yourself irritated, I would like you to realize that the anxiety is your psychological thermometer and that you should ask yourself, "What is irritating me? Did I feel irritated when I woke up this morning? Did I feel irritated when I left the house this morning?" Zero in on what caused the irritation, then decide if you should go back and resolve the problem or disregard what caused it and just convert the irritation into creative energy.

Priority Order

Your third method of resolving conflict at the roots is by setting priorities. Take your conflicting goals and arrange them in an order of priority. As an example, what is more important, family or money? Family is more important, and that is why money comes first! If you are going to have the things that you and your family deserve, then your major efforts must initially be to create a financial foundation for future success. Which is the better way to sell, by referral or cold canvassing? Referral selling is the best way, and that is why cold prospecting often must come first, so you can develop the contacts in order to get referrals.

Why do people have difficulty setting priorities? All too often the goals we should achieve immediately are the more difficult, causing us to skip them in order to find more comfortable areas to strive toward. At this time, arrange your goals in order of priority and decide which are most important, which can be achieved most quickly, and which can be reached with the least effort. Then, based on a combination of these factors, decide which goal you should be working toward immediately. Sometimes an important goal—such as always having ten appointments in advance—should be achieved first, regardless of the effort. Often, if telephone prospecting is too difficult, then any approach that will get you started will be worthwhile.

Compromise

The fourth method of resolving conflict is referred to as "giving of yourself," or compromise. This is where you achieve the goals of others as a means of eliminating conflicts that might exist with your family, friends, or business associates. You must be ready to compromise, particularly if the first three methods have failed. While *compromise* may sound like a negative word, you have to realize that you live and work in society and you must be willing to bend a little if it helps you to continue striving toward your goals. Often people have difficulty compromising because they have low self-acceptance and therefore are insecure when getting involved with others. When people are security-oriented it is difficult to compromise.

Drawing the Line

The fifth method of resolving conflict is the most difficult and should be applied only when, after the greatest effort, all previous methods have failed. This method is referred to as "drawing the line." When do you have to stop compromising and draw the line? When compromise would mean compromising your self-respect or your integrity. You cannot compromise your acceptance of yourself, for self-acceptance is your primary objective and should never be sacrificed. By understanding those conflicts which are causing anxiety and applying these five solutions, you should immediately be able to reduce the frustration and anxiety which are caused by conflict and thus to become more effective.

IV

Ego Defense Mechanisms

The third and last major cause of anxiety relates to ego defense mechanisms, sometimes referred to as the "games people play." As a matter of background, each of us has weak spots within his ego that cause him to feel vulnerable. As an example, a new salesman starts his first day by calling on professional people during the morning. He gets a very poor response but—though discouraged—has the enthusiasm of a new salesman, so he continues to prospect in the afternoon. This time he calls on apartment houses, primarily occupied by young married couples, and gets a few good appointments. He comes back at the end of the first day claiming, "I can sell to newlyweds but I cannot sell to businessmen." Now, can a decision like this be made in a day? Probably not, but it could happen in a few days. Why does it happen so quickly?

When you begin selling, you are very anxious to discover your strengths in order to capitalize on them and to discover where you are not as qualified in order to avoid further failure and anxiety. Because of these factors you are overly sensitive to your first experiences and allow your initial reactions to overly influence your future behavior. In what aspect of your selling do you find yourself confident, and in what areas do you find yourself particularly defensive? In real estate, some salesmen see themselves as very good listers and others as good sellers. In selling office equipment, some salesmen feel very confident with certain product lines and very unsure with others.

Activity Games

If your wife wants you to clean out the garage, you may agree verbally, but you may hear a voice within you saying, "Are you a garage cleaner? You are a professional. You don't clean out garages." You do not see yourself as a garage cleaner, so how do you avoid doing it? There are two kinds of games you can play, lazy games and busy games. If you find yourself sleeping late, watching a football game, or taking extra time with breakfast, then you are playing lazy games. If all of a sudden you have a great deal of work to do, such as at the office or something you enjoy doing around the house, like mowing the lawn, then you are playing busy games. Either way you are avoiding that which you feel uncomfortable doing, regardless of what method you may be using or how you may appear as you avoid it.

How do you protect yourself from those responsibilities in your business that threaten you? Do you play lazy games, such as taking extra long lunch hours, getting started late, or playing golf on a Friday afternoon? Or do you play busy games, such as discussing with your manager what you should be doing, spending hours developing elaborate filing systems, sending out direct mail, studying the situation more extensively, but for some reason never productively achieving? Regardless of whether you appear busy or lazy, you are avoiding the situation and, in the final analysis, you may not become irritated by failure experiences but you will not achieve, and that can be most irritating of all.

People Games

While you will tend to play certain types of games in order to protect yourself from activities in which you feel vulnerable, there are other types of games you will play when dealing with people who you feel threaten you. While there are many types of defense mechanisms that you can use when handling people, the two major types are the empathy defense and the confidence defense.

Nice Guy Game

Empathy is initially a strength and includes such personality characteristics as sympathy, warmth, friendliness, receptiveness, humility, and emotional concern for others. Now how can these qualities help you in selling? You quickly establish rapport because people feel you are concerned about them. They do not mind answering your questions because you are so interested in them and you quickly discover what their needs are. You then go on to present solutions to them, but what happens when it comes time to close? What is more important to the empathetic salesman, the rapport or the money, the love or the signature? All too often the empathetic salesman is more concerned about the rapport than the signature. At this particular point, rather than closing, he will fall back on his empathy and continue to develop more rapport. Instead of closing he will start playing the "nice guy" game. Finally a letter is written to the manager: "Dear Mr. Manager, I want you to know what a wonderful pleasure it was dealing with your salesman. You are a credit to the community, and to your industry as well, for hiring people of his caliber; and just because we bought from another company should be no reflection on your salesman's ability." Because he was afraid to fail, he did fail; and because he protected himself by playing empathetic games, he was rejected empathetically. If you find people apologizing for buying from someone else, you are probably playing the empathetic game and not being as decisive as you should be for fear that you might be rejected.

Confidence Game

Now for the salesman who plays the confidence game—a different kind of confidence game from the one you know. Initially, confidence is an asset and includes such characteristics as aggressiveness, positiveness, and strength. With these qualities the salesman quickly takes the initiative, gains appointments, and makes presentations; but then it comes time to close. What if he is afraid to close for fear he might fail? How does he protect himself? If he uses his confidence as a defense, he will become even more confident and aggressive. He will tell you, "A sale begins with a close, it ends with a close, and you are closing everywhere in between because the prospect has money in his pocket and that money belongs to you." He keeps on closing until he has the order, and then he asks for three referrals. The customer is afraid to turn this salesman loose on any of his friends unless he might think of someone he does not like, and then he will give a referral. The following morning the salesman wonders why there is a message telling him that the customer has canceled the order. When he returns the call, he discovers that an unlisted number has just been put in, and he never does find that customer again. This defense is effective in the sense that it quickly gains sales, but there is often a loss in relationship as well as in sales.

Enthusiasm Game

A third defense mechanism is the enthusiasm game, which includes humor. With enthusiasm and humor the salesman creates an excitement for the product and gains the order. If he confronts any objections, he just becomes more excited until the prospect becomes overwhelmed by the salesman's strong enthusiasm for the product. The following morning, the customer calls up asking, "Could you please tell me what I bought yesterday?" The customer often has a case of buyer's remorse because he got so excited about what he was buying that he was never really sure why he wanted it and then questioned his decision.

Composure Game

A fourth defense is the composure game, which also includes the analytical and competence games. With composure and competence the salesman quickly gains the confidence of the prospect because he seems so deliberate and poised in his cool, intellectual approach. The prospect, for these reasons, becomes relaxed and receptive to what the salesman has to say and will invariably agree with the salesman's rational presentation. At the same time, because the salesman never gets particularly excited, neither does the prospect. While the salesman may gain agreement that his product will do all the things he claims it will, his lack of enthusiasm may keep the prospect from ever getting excited enough to buy. If the salesman realizes he is losing control because he is not getting the prospect excited, he may become more uptight, therefore projecting even more composure and getting farther away from the actual sale.

Which type of person do you prefer most of all—an individual who is empathetic, aggressive, enthusiastic, or competent? Which one do you prefer second of all, and which least of all? Now, how do your preferences relate to your own personality and the impact you create on others?

Ask people you work and live with—who know you well and would answer you objectively—how you seem to react when challenged or irritated by other people. Do you become more empathetic, more aggressive, more enthusiastic, or more competent? In the same order, but in different words, do you become more sensitive, more positive, more humorous, or more relaxed?

Number the personality types by what you		
	prefer in others	believe you project
Warm and empathetic	_____	_____
Aggressive and positive	_____	_____
Enthusiastic and humorous	_____	_____
Composed and competent	_____	_____

You should not be critical of yourself if you play games, for if you do not have defense mechanisms and people start threatening you, then you will start feeling vulnerable and find yourself motivated to avoid or possibly overreact. For this reason, if people claim that— instead of becoming more empathetic, aggressive, enthusiastic, or competent—you seem to become quiet and play back, then that indicates you will be motivated to withdraw because you have no protective devices to use when people challenge you. It is with these thoughts in mind that we realize how ego defense mechanisms can cause anxiety in either of two ways.

If you do not play games you can be hurt easily because you have no method of protecting yourself from the hostility of others, and that causes frustration. As an example, on one of my first days of selling for IBM in the garment section in New York, I called on a particular office where I was met by a very pleasant looking receptionist. I introduced myself by saying, "My name is Art Mortell, and I am with IBM. We have some new products that can completely revolutionize your whole office operations. If I can show your boss a way of increasing his office production by 50 percent, do you think he would give me fifteen minutes of his time?"

She then said, "Get the ————— out of here."

It took a number of days for my ego to heal as I was not yet conditioned to that kind of experience. Gradually, I began to learn certain games to play which got me beyond such problems. Over a period of time I became conditioned to regard this kind of experience as normal, though at first the lack of defense mechanisms caused me considerable frustration.

At the same time, strong defense mechanisms can cause frustration for another reason: They can cut you off from the kind of involvement you need in order to succeed. As an example, one of the salesmen with whom I worked at IBM tried to help me by telling me, "Art, you have to protect yourself at all times. People are basically bad. You have to expect the worst, because you will usually get it. Be suspicious at all times. It's a dog-eat-dog world; it is vicious out there. You have to do unto others before they do you in." No one could ever reject this salesman, but then he never gained the kind of involvement that allowed him to succeed to the degree he should have.

Do you tend to be underprotecting and hurt easily or overprotecting and not gain involvement you need? Either way there will be frustration. As an analogy, imagine knights in tournament during the medieval period. Imagine a knight getting onto his horse with a lance, clad only in his underwear. If you asked him why he was wearing no armor, he might tell you, "I do not believe in playing games and protecting myself. I am honest and open and do not need defense mechanisms." That man is in deep trouble. At the same time, though, his opponent may be so well protected that his shield is too heavy to let him lift his arm. His helmet not only covers his head but his eyes as well, and his armor is so heavy that, when he finally gets on his horse, the horse collapses. He isn't going anywhere. Again, which way do you tend to go? Are you underprotected or overprotected? When you do play games, what kind of games do you play? Do they protect you from getting hurt? Do they allow you to get involved? Do they help you to achieve? Do they threaten people? How *effective* are they?

Effective Game Playing

You need the *right kind* of defense mechanism, one that allows you to get totally involved with people and at the same time protects you from hostility. How can you do both and achieve your objectives, all at the same time? In order to develop the best defense, we need to take the best qualities of our two primary defense mechanisms, the empathy defense and the confidence defense. First, what is it you like about the empathetic individual? He is very pleasant and emotionally concerned about people. But what is it you dislike about him? He lacks the persistence and decisiveness a salesman needs to achieve objectives and be productive. Now, what do you like about the confident individual? He gets the job done, he is productive and action-oriented; but what do you dislike about him? He tends to come on too strong and does not project the sensitivity for people's feelings which is so important in interpersonal relationships. Now take the best of each and put them together and you have a *decisively sensitive individual,* someone who is *constantly persistent* in an *empathetic way.* Now how do you achieve this objective?

Rebound with Empathy

The first step is to get totally and emotionally involved. This is easy to do if you know you cannot be irritated; and I can assure you that because of the next three steps you will feel protected. If the prospect or whomever you might be dealing with becomes hostile, do not take it personally. Instead, be objective. If you disengage yourself emotionally from the situation, it will not bother you; but as long as you are taking it personally, you will be oversensitive and have difficulty developing any creative solutions. Once your are objective, the third step becomes easy, and that is developing a solution which will resolve the challenge confronting you. And then the fourth step is to rebound with empathy.

These four steps may seem rather academic to you, and for that reason I would like to present a number of practical examples which will make it meaningful. The first example I do not recommend, but it is worth presenting for one reason. A real estate salesman was "door knocking" in an effort to find people who might be interested in listing their homes with him. He knocked on one door and introduced himself in a pleasant, honest, open way; and the homeowner, without a word, slammed the door in his face. The salesman, as he walked away, realized that the homeowner had irritated him so badly that he would not be able to prospect for the rest of the day. He would probably go to sleep depressed that night because of having accomplished nothing for the day, probably have bad dreams, and wake up the next morning even more depressed. He realized that he could not allow this to happen to him, so he went back to the door and rang the bell again. As he heard the homeowner coming to the door he picked up the man's flowerpot, and as the door was opened he said, "Don't ever do that to me again." With that he released the flowerpot, smashed it in front of the man, and gave him his card and walked away. This man called up the real estate salesman afterwards, apologized to him for being rude, and gave him a referral for a listing which he then went on to sell. I certainly would not recommend this technique to anybody, but the salesman did not stay depressed.

The next example I *would* recommend. A salesman was door knocking in a personable and honest way. He knocked on one door and, after introducing himself, the woman slammed the door in his face. As he stood there he realized that he had done nothing to deserve such a reaction and that he could not take her hostility personally because she did not even know him. With that he thought of a creative solution, walked around the house, and knocked on the back door. She came to the door and asked, "Now what do you want?" He replied, "Well, the lady at the front door was kind of rude to me, so I thought I would call on the lady at the back door, and find out what she was like." He had developed the ability to rebound with empathy.

In another example, a real estate salesman who was very reserved and empathetic was door knocking for listings when he came across a hostile homeowner who yelled at him, "All real estate salesmen are crooks." Before this quiet and sensitive real estate salesman realized what he was doing he had thrown open his suit jacket and yelled back, "Do you see a gun, do you see a gun?" He then realized that this was not his personality and he felt very foolish; but it was too late—the homeowner was already laughing. A few minutes later the man admitted why he had been hostile. Three years previously he had taken the real estate exam and failed. The real estate salesman had learned two important lessons within a few minutes: If you come back at people with empathy or humor you can disarm their hostility, and you will often discover that their hostility has nothing to do with you.

These concepts can apply to any situation in life. As an example, I was conducting a workshop program for a group of computer salesmen, and they each had written down one statement from someone in any area of their life that could irritate them. I would then read back each one of these statements, and the first salesman who could respond would gain a point; if the response was with empathy, there was an additional point; if with humor, a third point; and if in question form, a fourth point. A salesman could therefore score as many as four points, and the idea of the game was to help the salesmen to react better to challenging situations. In this one particular session one salesman had written, "The one thing that can irritate me is when my wife says, 'you do not give me enough of your time and you are not sensitive to me.' " I read this one irritant to the group and one salesman responded, "O.K. darling, I have ten seconds, why do you feel that way?"

I have four children and I have succeeded in helping them to become persistent. Of course, I often pay for this, as when they go to bed. They have developed an almost infinite number of techniques to stay up. As an example, Johnny goes to bed and a few minutes later says, "Daddy, can I have a glass of water?"

I reply, "You've already had three glasses of water and two glasses of milk, now go to sleep."

A few minutes later, I hear, "Daddy, can I have a glass of water?"

"If you're not quiet, I'm going to get a belt and come in there and spank you."

A few minutes later, "Daddy, when you bring the belt, could you bring a glass of water?"

The child has won, because he merges the persistence of the confident individual with the style of the empathetic personality. If I had to figure any one reason why salesmen do not succeed, it is because, when people irritate them, they do not come back. Your ability to come back, particularly with empathy, is one of your primary objectives.

What Type Are You?

If you want to change, you should first understand which kind of personality you are. The first test that might help you determine whether you are the empathetic or the confident type requires some familiarity with the *Peanuts* comic strip. If you had to make a choice, which personality would you prefer to be, Charlie Brown or Lucy? If you select Charlie Brown, then you are the empathetic type; and if you select Lucy, you are the confident type. If you still are not sure which type of person you tend to be, then which kind of relationship with people do you prefer—a pleasant one-to-one relationship or one in which you are in control? If you prefer a one-to-one type of relationship where you have a pleasant give and take, then you are an empathetic type of person. If you prefer to control, you are the aggressive, confident type of person.

A third test: What do you feel are your major strengths with people, particularly in selling? The empathetic person will answer, "My major strength with people is the fact that I like people and people like me. I am able to develop rapport rapidly and I enjoy helping people. I am good at discovering what their needs are and I like to help people solve their problems." This is an empathetic individual who will do a good job of developing rapport, discovering needs, and presenting solutions; but when it comes time to close, his oversensitivity for rapport—and his need to be liked—will invariably reduce his effectiveness in being decisive and getting the order. How will the aggressive, confident type of salesman answer the same question? "I am good in selling because I enjoy directing people and getting them to agree with me. I enjoy the challenge of persuading people to my way of thinking. I like to get results." This individual *will* get results, but he will often create a negative impact on others in terms of threatening them. This may cause them to avoid him, resulting in lost orders and poor customer relations as well as poor relations with associates. Again, *the ability to merge the persistence and action-orientation of the aggressive, confident salesman with the warmth and friendliness of the empathetic person will create the kind of balance that is referred to as charisma:* the merging of opposite characteristics into a personality with which virtually everybody can identify.

Why Not Change?

While you probably would like to gain this kind of balance, you may not *want* to change, even though you may agree that the balancing of empathy with persistence is important. There are specific reasons why empathetic people do not want to become aggressive and why aggressive people do not want to become empathetic. First the empathetic individual. Why doesn't he want to become aggressive? How does he describe the aggressive individual but as someone who is insensitive, high pressure, and obnoxious? Now what happens if someone starts to pressure him? He will turn that person off; and what would happen if he were to become aggressive with someone who felt *he* was pressuring? What might the person do to him? Possibly turn *him* off or reject him. The most important objective of our empathetic individual is to be liked, and the worst experience is to be rejected. Therefore, he will scrupulously avoid projecting any characteristics that may cause rejection or loss of acceptance. It is not that he lacks aggressiveness, decisiveness, or strength, but that he actually stifles such characteristics.

Now for our aggressive, confident type of salesman. Why does he suppress sympathy for others? How does he describe the sensitive, warm, sympathetic individual? As weak; and if he were to project sympathy and people thought him weak, what might they do to him? They might take advantage of him. And what is the major objective of the confident type of individual? It is to control, and the worse experience is to lose control or be dominated. If he projects empathy and people think he is weak, they might take advantage of him and he will lose control. This is the reason why he does not like empathy. He literally avoids it.

The empathetic individual should not allow his excessive need for acceptance from others to cut him off from the kind of decisiveness that will help him to succeed and also help his customers meet their objectives. He has to realize that people do not invite him to their businesses or homes to build up his ego by liking him but because they assume there may be some way he may help them. By not asking them to make a decision, he does not help them resolve their problems or satisfy their needs. Equally, the aggressive, confident type of salesman should not allow his value system, which is based on needing control, to cut him off from the kind of emotional involvement that will allow him to help people as well as to meet his own objectives. Certainly you need games—but you need the right kind.

Take the situation of an aggressive, confident salesman who does very well financially but tends to threaten people. As he begins to make a considerable amount of money, he looks around for a new challenge and decides to go into management. His company, although impressed with his sales ability, has been displeased with the negative impact that he creates on others. They have overlooked some of the negative reactions of his customers and associates, but they are reluctant to put him in charge of salesmen. It is more expensive to lose a good salesman than a good customer. Nevertheless, he threatens to join a competitor unless he gets a management position, so they decide to give him a try. Within a few weeks he has lost almost every salesman, as they have either quit or transferred to another office.

Still, over a period of time, he gradually attracts people to him who either identify with him or follow his instructions and succeed, even though they do not necessarily like him. Gradually he develops the most successful sales office in the company—and then decides he needs a new challenge. He wants to become a regional manager. Now the company was willing to lose some customers because of his strong techniques, and they suffered through a period of high turnover when he became a manager, but they were not going to risk losing managers because of him. This would be too expensive. They tell him, "If only you had some feeling for people. If only you were sensitive, we would be willing to take a chance with you. If you want to become a regional vice-president then you have to go to Big Sur and join an encounter seminar, a sensitivity training program. Maybe this will give you the concern for others that will allow us to put you in that position."

Our manager thinks, "The last thing in the world I want to do is spend a weekend with long-haired freaks and mixed-up psychologists. I've heard of these touchie-feelie sessions, everyone touching each other, but if that is what I have to go through to become a regional vice-president then I'll put up with it for a few days."

He drives into Big Sur and soon finds himself in a twenty-four hour group session with eleven introverts who spend the first hours talking about very little, with the leader saying nothing. Finally our manager, chafing from lack of action, explodes: "What the blazes are we *here* for? Are we going to spend twenty-four hours just staring at each other and chitchatting? I've got more important things to do than this."

Eleven introverts for the first time in their lives unite, asking him, "What's eating *you?* Why do you have to come in here and try to dominate us? What is *your* problem?"

"What do you mean *my* problem? The problem in this world is that there are too many dingalings and flakes like you and not enough guts ballplayers like me!" But there are eleven of them and only one of him, and the hours go by.

Finally, by the tenth hour, he admits that the reason he comes across so strongly is because he is unsure of himself, and the more unsure of himself he is the more confident he sounds. But they aren't satisfied. They want to know why he is like this, and by the twentieth hour he finally admits that when he was nine years old his mother allowed him to go out into the street and play with the kids next door, and they all began to beat him. In his desperate effort to get home he, by mistake, ran over one of them, and they all panicked and ran away from him. "And I haven't stopped running over people since then." By the twenty-fourth hour they have him as warm and sensitive as he was at the age of nine.

Monday morning he comes into the office to conduct his weekly sales meeting announcing: "Fellows, you're beautiful. I've missed all of you during these last few days. I want you to know how great it is to be back with you, I love you all." From that day on his tremendous warmth and sympathy create a fantastic impact on his people. He never has turnover. He has the finest morale in the company, and his office is one big warm, happy family.

Of course, production falls, profits disappear, and finally the company has to disband the office. They can't bring themselves to fire him because everyone loves him, so they claim that the production in that particular area has gone down for a lack of market —and besides, they need the office for storage space.

His problem was not that he was playing the wrong game by being aggressive and confident but that he was not adding certain qualities to the game he *was* playing to make it as totally effective as it could be. Where are *you?* What qualities do *you* need to add to your present defense mechanism that will allow you to be more effective in any given situation?

In conclusion, you need to be able to resolve anxiety at the roots by eliminating the causes of anxiety or converting anxiety into creative energy. You can eliminate anxiety at the roots by changing your attitudes toward failure so your fears do not affect you. You have to tune your expectations into reality and realize that often you have to *feel* successful when you are failing most of the time. You have to learn how to resolve conflict at the roots. You have to develop the right kind of defense mechanisms in which you get totally involved with people *but still protect yourself by knowing how to come back in a disarming way.* If you do not do these things, you will at least convert the resulting anxiety into a force for achievement by developing those techniques that get rid of anxiety *creatively* within every major area of your life: physical, financial, family, and personal.

V

The Challenge to Change

I would like you to imagine a salesman who finds his acceptance within himself and therefore is not oversensitive to the reactions of others while in the process of achieving his goals. When he faces a situation in which he has never succeeded before, he has the right attitude toward possible failure or rejection. His expectations are realistic. He resolves conflict at the roots. He becomes totally involved with people, and if they threaten him he rebounds with empathy. When he does not do these things, he at least converts the resulting anxiety into creative energy. Now what is going to happen to someone who does most of these things most of the time? He will succeed, but to what extent?

He will not go as far as he wants. We have enough examples of salesmen who, while having all the ability and skills necessary to reach $25,000 to $50,000 per year, for some reason, when reaching $1,000 or $1,500 per month, level off and go no further.

Have you ever experienced a particularly successful month and then for some reason just seemed to waste the next month—or watched other salesmen have this type of experience? Sure, you would like to make more money, but for some reason, once you can pay your bills for the month, you are no longer excited about keeping the momentum going. What is the problem?

It is not based so much on lack of ability. We all know people who do not have any unusual intellectual ability and still reach significant levels of financial success in selling. A salesman's achievement is not based on his wants or even on his ability but on what he *believes* he is worth.

As an example, I once worked with a salesman who would make $6,000 one month and the following month nothing. It took him an entire month, he explained, to handle all the paperwork in order to make sure that the sales went through properly; but on the third month he would zero again, and that month he could not explain. He did not know why he seemed disinterested in the business in the third month, would sleep late, and did not particularly care what occurred. In the fourth month he would earn $6,000 again and then zero two more months in a row. I asked him what his goal for the year was and he said, "Twenty-five thousand. I made it last year and I am on target to make it this year." I agreed with him, because he had the ability, after making $6,000 in a month, to zero two months in a row *and get himself right back down to what he believed he was worth.*

I once worked with another salesman who was making $200 per month, and I tried to discover what his problem was. I learned that his wife was working and that his bills were $1,200 per month. How much was his wife making per month? She was a nurse making $1,000 per month; and he was supplementing her income. It is disturbing to realize how often a salesman will earn only enough to pay his bills, and if he has a pension or his wife is working then it is just that much less he needs. If he becomes more effective in selling and can therefore accomplish his goals more quickly, he often does not attempt to increase his income but rather spends the extra time playing golf or just sleeping late. I am contending that even if you have the ability to handle failure, rejection, and anxiety, you will only earn as much as you believe you are worth.

Your Feeling of Self-worth

Is it hard for you to believe that people do not achieve what they want nor what they are able to accomplish, but rather what they believe they are worth, their image of themselves? If you were to put this book in your left hand, do you think that you would be able to lift it with your right hand? Of course. But can you stretch out between two chairs, the back of your head on one chair, your heels on the other, nothing supporting you underneath, and have two people sit on top of your stomach and chest? You may not believe that you can, but haven't you seen this done in a stage show, in a theatrical act, or on television? You probably have, and therefore you believe it can be done. If you believe it can be done, then why are you unable to do it without hypnosis?

It is because, while you may intellectually believe it can be done, you do not see yourself, in terms of self-image, being able to achieve it. Yet under hypnosis you could be told, "You are straight as a board, as rigid as a piece of steel." You could then be stretched out between two chairs, your head on one chair, your feet on the other, nothing supporting you underneath, and have two people actually sit on top of your stomach and chest and you would be able to hold them. Then, thirty seconds later, the hypnotist could have you stand up, and while you were still under hypnosis, he would say, "you cannot lift this book." Your muscles would strain and the perspiration would break out on your forehead, but you could not budge the book, because people do not operate according to their ability or according to what they want, *but only according to what they believe they can accomplish.*

It is your image of yourself that determines your income as well as every aspect of your behavior. It determines how you project to others, how you handle anxiety, which products you feel you can sell comfortably and with which you feel uncomfortable, whom you enjoy dealing with and whom you avoid.

Comfort Versus Change

For this reason your success in the future is directly related to your ability to change or improve your self-image. Before we can discuss how this can be achieved, we must first examine the reason people have so much difficulty changing. First, I am going to make a statement that will probably surprise you: Man's most basic need is comfort. This may be hard to believe, but the need to be comfortable is actually even more important than the basic need to survive! The individual who becomes too uncomfortable will often sacrifice survival and even commit suicide in order to eliminate this discomfort. Further, you will find that you are motivated primarily by anxiety. As an example, you do not go to sleep when you are tired, but only when you are irritated because of being tired and wish to eliminate the irritation. You do not eat when you are hungry but only when you are irritated because you are hungry and wish to eliminate the irritation. In fact, experimenters have discovered that part of the rat's brain which triggers anxiety when the rat is hungry. When they removed that small section of the brain and put food in front of the rat, the rodent starved to death because as it became hungry it never became irritated.

In addition, it does not really bother you when you cannot pay the bills, you are on the verge of being fired, orders are being canceled, and your family has left you. What bothers you is the *anxiety* these things cause. The "hippie" culture today is based on the fact that so many young people would rather be comfortable right now than struggle to gain those things that might possibly make them comfortable in the future. To repeat: Man's most basic need is to be in a state of equilibrium, to be comfortable, and to avoid anxiety. Now what is the relationship between this basic need to be comfortable and man's difficulty in changing?

Two Personalities

Before answering the last question, there is one more fact which we must understand, and that is the fact that man is a split personality. This might sound like a threatening thought, but man actually has two personalities. You have two voices within you, two separate images. To prove this to yourself, imagine a salesman who is about to try something he has failed at many times before. What does his negative self-image say? "You can't do it. Remember last time? Why would you want to try again? All you will do is fail again." What does the positive self-image say? "Well, let's try once more." The salesman tries again and he fails again. What does his negative self-image say? "I told you so. Why didn't you listen to me in the first place? You know you can't do it." What does the positive self-image say? It may not say anything, because it has given up, which would be unfortunate. One hopes it may say, "Well, at least I tried." The salesman tries again and this time he succeeds. What does his negative self-image say? "Lucky. Better stop while you're ahead because if you do try again you will only fail and lose what you have." What does the positive self-image say? "I can do it. In fact I'll make it two in a row!"

Change and Anxiety

Yes, there are two separate voices within your mind; and every time you try to do something you're not sure of, you'll hear these two voices arguing back and forth. Now, what will that internal conflict do? It will cause anxiety, which destroys your basic need to be comfortable. In conclusion, it is change that causes internal argument, which causes anxiety, which destroys your basic need to be comfortable and therefore motivates you to *avoid* change and stay in a state of equilibrium, to remain comfortable.

Then why do we find that people change frequently up until the age of fifteen or eighteen? While there may be many reasons why people change frequently during their youth, the primary reason is that they were forced into change. Imagine back to childhood when you had to give a speech in school and your knees began to shake and the last thing in the world that you wanted to do was give that speech. Then why did you do it? Your teacher told you that if you did not you would fail the course. She made you do it. When you did not want to clean your room, you did it for the same reason. Your parents threatened you. You were told what would happen if you did not do it, and the threats caused so much anxiety that in order to stay comfortable you had to change.

The reason why you may have done certain things in the military, on a sports team, or in peer groups is usually the same. Why do you begin smoking when smoking causes irritation and makes you ill? Because if you do not learn how to smoke you will be rejected by others, and that anxiety is worse than the discomfort caused by learning how to smoke. Today you may not be changing as frequently as you did in childhood, not because you've lost the ability to change but because no one is forcing you to change. To continue to change requires that you become your own teacher, parent, or manager. You need to manage yourself, and this often means forcing yourself into success patterns. You need to *make yourself* change.

Appreciating Your Potential

To do this requires that you first appreciate your potential. Watch what happens if you do not appreciate your potential and for some reason you try and fail. You will tend to say to yourself, "I guess that proves I shouldn't have tried in the first place." This will cause your initial doubts to convert into negative convictions, which will motivate you to avoid trying again. If, instead, you appreciate your potential and you fail, you will say, "Something went wrong, because I deserve to succeed. This means I will have to try twice as hard the next time, or try a step at a time, try from a different direction, or ask somebody to help me; because I deserve to succeed and I am not going to allow this failure to stop me." The appreciation of your potential has a dramatic impact on how you handle failure.

Babe Ruth was once in a bad hitting slump when he was asked by a reporter, "What are you doing to get out of this slump?" Babe replied, "I'm not doing anything to get out of the slump because it is not my problem. I'm not going to get upset. It's that pitcher's problem out there. He is the one who is going to suffer."

The appreciation of your potential also has a dramatic impact on how you handle success. If you do not appreciate your potential and you do succeed, you will say to yourself, "I feel fortunate to have gotten this far. This means I can take a rest and enjoy it for awhile." If, instead, you appreciate your potential and you succeed, you will then say, "This is a steppingstone to greater levels of achievement. It is just an example of what I can really accomplish in my next effort." The appreciation of your potential has a dramatic impact on how you handle both failure and success experiences in life. It is with this in mind that I would like you to give some thought to the tremendous potential that you have.

Memory and Self-image

The first example may sound negative initially, but sometime around the age of thirty you begin to lose approximately 100,000 brain cells permanently each day. This means that you will lose 1 million brain cells every ten days, 3 million per month, 36 million per year, 360 million in the next ten years, and 1 billion brain cells will be permanently lost in the next thirty years. You may feel you have only a few days left to go, but the brain starts out with twelve billion cells; and at the rate of 100,000 net loss per day it takes thirty years just to lose 8 percent of your capacity! Yet with this phenomenal brain capacity we have people making such statements as, "I have a very bad memory for names." Have you ever said it?

Yet under hypnosis you could recall the first and last names of every child in your first grade of grammar school, and by the correct chair. If you believe that you cannot, you will not be able to; and equally, if you believe that you can, you will find certain names starting to come to you. The memory is there, but it is your self-image that determines if you will gain access to it.

An example of a negative self-image regarding memory is the story of a minister who thought he had a bad memory for names, and whenever he had to recall names he used to put them on a piece of paper inside his suit jacket. One Sunday morning he was giving a sermon on the Creation, and he said, "And God created the first man and his name was . . ." and he looked into his jacket and then turned to the congregation, "Adam. And he created the first woman, and her name was . . ." and he looked into his jacket again, and turning to the congregation, "Eve. And they had a son and his name was . . ." He then opened his jacket again, and turning to the congregation, "Robert Hall." You may often fail in life, but invariably it will not be for a lack of ability as much as it will be for a lack of believing in yourself.

Just Do It

The next example that illustrates the phenomenal potential that people have is one that you are probably familiar with under different circumstances, because it has happened so many times. It is about a girl 5 feet, 4 inches tall and weighing 110 pounds who looked out the window and saw that the car had slipped off the jack and fallen on her father. She ran outside, lifted the front of the car, pulled her father out, and drove him to the hospital. Now, how was she able to do it? If she had asked herself if she could do it she would have said no and would not have been able to. She was able to save her father because she did not think about it. She just did it. Maybe your main problem is that once knowing what you *should* do, you ask yourself if you *can* do it. Then a little voice says no, and you don't. Stop thinking and do it!

A similar situation is that of a man who, as a young boy, had to leave school because it was the Depression and his family needed the money; so he sold shoelaces on a street corner. In his twenties he had saved enough money to be able to open a small retail store. In his thirties he opened a major department store; in his forties he began to open up stores nationally; and in his fifties he was a multimillionaire. One day he was asked, "What do you attribute your success to? You have all this wealth, and yet no educational background. Why do you feel you have done so well?"

He responded, "It is very simple. I buy it for one dollar, I sell it for two dollars, and I'm happy with one percent." The problem with too many people is that they know too much. *They have the unfortunate ability to figure out why every idea might not work for them, thus justifying their failure even to try in the first place.* Again, we find that very often our most successful people are those people who do not think too much. They just act!

To See Yourself in the Future

The way you should approach yourself is best illustrated by Aristotle. He would show his students an acorn and ask, "What do you see?" They would respond, "We see an acorn, what are we supposed to see?" And he would challenge them, "Do you see the acorn, or do you see what the acorn can become—the beautiful oak tree?" That is the challenge to you today: When you look at yourself, what do you see? Do you see yourself as you are, or as what you can become?

What did Grandma Moses see in herself at the age of seventy-eight? She had never painted in her life. If she had seen herself as an old lady getting ready to die she would not have been starting anything new. Rather, she saw herself growing young, and twenty years later she was a famous artist.

Colonel Sanders is another example. During the Depression he had the courage to start his own business, a gas station. This was not the gas company's investment but his own. As the years went by he opened and expanded a restaurant in the back of his gas station; and in 1955, at the age of sixty-five and on the eve of retirement, he was worth $140,000. At this point, the state built a major road 7 miles away. Suddenly there was not enough traffic going by to support the high overhead expenses that were involved in the establishment he had built. Within a short period of time he was bankrupt and on social security. Now what did he see in himself; an old man who was bankrupt or a man starting a new career?

He took a recipe for fried chicken that he had used in his restaurant and began traveling across the country, cooking the chicken in the back of his car and trying to get restaurant people to taste it and agree with him that because of his eleven herbs and spices it was worth a percentage of whatever they sold in chicken. Imagine yourself owning a restaurant. It is around the lunch hour, and you are very busy, when an old man comes in and says to you, "Hey, I've got this chicken in the back of my car that I just cooked. I would like you to come out and taste a thigh or a leg and agree with me that because of my herbs and spices it is worth a percentage of whatever you sell for the rest of your life." You look out the window and see a dirty old car that has traveled hundreds of miles in the last few days. Now how turned on would you be to taste the old man's chicken in the back of that car? Three years later at the age of sixty-eight, Colonel Sanders had two restaurants that were supplementing his social security benefits; but seven years later, at the age of seventy-five, Colonel Sanders sold his fried chicken for a finger-lickin' fifteen million dollars. If he had seen himself at the age of sixty-five as a defeated, bankrupt old man, then that is what he would be today. Instead, he saw himself not as he was but as what he could become. That is the reason he was willing to make sacrifices each day in order to get himself back to what he believed he was worth. It is this ability to see yourself in the future and say "That's where I *belong*" that will assure your success.

An excellent illustration of this concept is presented by Dr. Frankl in his book, *Man's Search for Meaning.** Dr. Frankl, a psychiatrist during World War II, was imprisoned in a concentration camp. While he was in the concentration camp, his fellow prisoners realized that there was one freedom that they had that could end the suffering of each day. It was the freedom to take their own lives, to commit suicide. To Dr. Frankl, as a psychiatrist as well as a fellow prisoner, it became a personal challenge to keep these men alive. Now what could he say to a man that would help him to live through that suffering each day—to make the suffering not only tolerable but actually in some cases meaningful? Finally he found

---

* *Man's Search for Meaning*, Washington Square Press, N.Y. (1963).

the answer in a single question. He would ask, "What is the first thing that you are going to do when you get out?" One man said, "To finish my manuscript," another man said, "To see my son again." All at once they realized the relationship between the suffering and where they wanted to be: that if the more they suffered the closer they came to where they wanted to be, then it could be called not suffering but only part of the process of becoming. Surely, if this ability to see oneself in the future could help them endure such suffering, then it can help you whenever you find yourself depressed or upset in life. See yourself not as you are *but as you can become.*

The Extent of Human Potential

Here you might say, "Yes, positive thinking can help you make better use of your potential, but there are a lot of things you *can't* do, no matter how much positive thinking you use." Agreed. In fact, I used to give a lecture in which I would talk about the fact that if you had the desire to be a surgeon, had the ability to be a surgeon, and you were willing to learn how to be a surgeon, that still did not mean that you could go home that night and cut up your spouse unless you had the skills to be a surgeon (or a sudden desire for travel—up the river). Then, on one particular day, a student interrupted me and asked, "Then what about the great imposter?" I was not familiar with the *great imposter** at that time so I read the book by that name and I recommend that you read it.

The great imposter, Ferdinand Walpo Demara, was motivated to take on the roles of other people. On one particular occasion he decided to become a psychologist, so he went through college catalogues until he came across the name of a Dr. French who had a very fine background, with many college degrees. Here was the kind of person Demara wanted to be, so he decided to become Dr. French. He wrote letters under a false business letterhead to each of the colleges that Dr. French had graduated from, claiming that his company was interested in hiring Dr. French as an industrial psychologist and that he needed the doctor's transcripts to finalize the decision. Within a few days he received the transcripts and then mailed them to a small college in Pennsylvania that was looking for a psychology professor. The Pennsylvania college was very impressed that anyone with his background would be interested in a position in their humble college, and for the small income that they would pay. When Demara arrived at the college, the job was as

---

* *The Great Imposter,* Random House, N.Y. (1959).

good as his. The only question was what title he would have. He suggested "Chairman of the Department of Philosophy." One year later, bored, he resigned. Merely reading the textbook the night before the class kept him a few hours ahead of the students and therefore did not offer the challenge he needed.

He therefore went back to New England where he was born, met a Canadian-born surgeon, and stole his transcripts. He then went to Canada, where he had never been before, and applied to the Queen's Navy for a post as a doctor. They were deeply impressed that a Canadian-born surgeon would return to Canada to accept a position for such a humble income. He was assigned to a hospital and soon found himself incompetent, as he had no background, training, or skills in medicine. He therefore approached the doctor in charge of the hospital and explained to him that, since it was the Korean War, there were Canadian sergeants in Korea who often found themselves in charge of men who were ill, and that they would have no idea how serious the illness was or what to do about it. He suggested that something be written that would be an easy guide for a field sergeant to refer to in order to make decisions regarding illnesses. The doctor was so impressed with the value of the idea that within forty-eight hours he had written and printed a brochure outlining the major illnesses, what to look for, and what to do about them. From this point on our great imposter went through the hospital diagnosing the patients by referring to this printed material. If the symptoms were not described in the material, then it had to mean that it was an unusual problem, and such cases generally require another professional opinion. He would ask an associate doctor, "This looks rather unusual, what do you think?" With such techniques the great imposter was able to meet and conquer any situation.

He needed a new challenge, and asked for a more difficult assignment; so they put him on a ship to Korea. He was the only doctor on board. On one of his first days off Korean waters a small South Korean ship came alongside the Canadian vessel with nineteen wounded soldiers. On that day he had to perform nineteen separate operations without any surgical skills, background, training, or reading on the subject. Demara prepared himself for the ordeal by first drinking a sufficient quantity of rum. He then took out a book on surgery that he had never had to open before, went through the instructions page by page, and successfully completed the nineteen operations.

Again he needed a new challenge, so he asked the commanding officer to put him ashore each day to bring medical attention to the villagers, and that is how he got caught. The Canadian government became so impressed with him and his efforts to help people that they began publishing articles about him. Because the articles were so well accepted, research on his background was done, and it was found that he had no background at all. I am not suggesting that you try to get ahead in such an unorthodox fashion and with such risks involved. Nevertheless, I am suggesting that possibly your major obstacle in life is selling yourself short. If you believe in yourself and are not afraid to try, you will achieve new levels of success.

Of course, the results aren't always beneficial to society. There was once a man who believed he could take over the world. He was a rabble-rouser, so they threw him in jail. While in jail he wrote a book outlining in detail how he was going to do it. If you had seen this man behind bars, with no background to speak of, writing a book on how he was going to conquer the world, you probably would not have even bothered laughing at him. Yet, six million people had to die to stop Adolf Hitler from achieving his goal, because that part of his mind which would have said, "Adolf, you are only a painter, you can't take over Germany, a nation of great people, of scientists, musicians, and artists," that part of his mind was missing. The part of his mind which would have said, "Adolf, you can't take over Estonia, Lithuania, Finland, Norway, Belgium, Luxembourg, Netherlands, France, Poland, Austria, Rumania, Czechoslovakia, Bulgaria, Yugoslavia, Italy, Greece, and Egypt," that part of his mind was missing, so he did it. For good or bad, when you do not question whether you can do it or not, you can often do unbelievable things!

Another example is presented in *Life* magazine's Science Library, in the particular book on the mind. They speak of an eleven-year-old boy who could play a thousand pieces of music by ear. If you gave him a date, such as November 11, 1805, he could tell you what day of the week it was, and at computerlike speeds. When famed memory expert Larry Lorayne performs the same feat at sales seminars, it draws gasps of amazement from the audience. Yet this boy could not go to school because his IQ was 50. His problem was that he had brain damage which had interfered with the functioning part of his brain that handles the decision-making process as well as the area where the self-image develops. He could not do what a normal child does, nor could he question what he could or could not do. Therefore parts of his brain that had not been damaged developed to such an extent that in some areas he was a genius! People generally have these same potential abilities but may lose access to them because of negative self-image.

If that part of the brain where self-image develops stops functioning either because of brain damage, mental illness, or some unusual motivation, the individual will not question himself. Instead he will accomplish virtually anything he desires if it is within his potential. Of course, it is good that we have a negative self-image in certain aspects of our life because it prevents us from doing those things that could hurt us or others. At the same time, our negative self-image often causes us to adapt to the mediocrity of others around us and reduces our ability to fulfill our potential and fully satisfy our needs for achievement and self-esteem. Thus the need to change our self-image in order to better capitalize on our potential.

To do this requires, first, that you understand the nature of your self-image.

VI

Self-image Psychology

Many people believe that personality is something that is set or fixed. Rather, we discover that personality is really a series of opinions that you have of yourself, of what you can or cannot do. I doubt that you are equally good at everything that you try to accomplish. Your ability at water skiing is probably different from your ability to learn languages, swim, sell, or conduct a conversation at a cocktail party. Instead, your self-image and your results vary from one responsibility or activity to another.

As an example, I would like you to imagine a salesman who has a good self-image with good results in such areas as working hard, knowledge of the business, ability to prospect and to develop rapport, ask questions, discover people's needs, develop solutions, follow up on prospects, convert anxiety into creative energy, balance persistence with empathy, and be well organized. There is only one negative area of this salesman's self-image, and that is his ability to close. This negative self-image may have originated in a fear of rejection, which has caused negative experiences when closing and culminated in a negative self-image. I am sure you will agree that for the lack of this one ability the others will be blocked or seriously reduced in effectiveness.

Now, is it possible that within your self-image there might be an area that is negative and is thus blocking you from capitalizing on your abilities? If so, it is crucial that you determine what aspect of your self-image is negative so that you can prepare yourself for change. In the next chapter you will be presented with twenty-four separate techniques for change that can create rapid and significant results for you. Nevertheless, these techniques have no value if you have nothing to apply them to. That's why it's important at this time to determine what aspect of your self-image may be negative, and therefore reducing your overall effectiveness.

Again, personality or self-image is a series of opinions that you have of yourself regarding what you can or cannot do. To change personality does not require changing the entire personality but just *one aspect of the personality.*

How Self-image Develops

Before we can discuss these techniques for change, you should first understand how you came to be the kind of person that you are today.

How does personality or self-image develop? How have you come to see yourself the way you are today? As an analogy, how has your physical image of yourself developed? You look in the mirror and you see a reflection of yourself, causing you to develop within your mind an image of what you look like physically. Now, do you see the mirror? You do not, because when you look in the mirror you do not look into it to see the mirror but only to see a reflection of yourself. Now, when you look at people, what do you see? What I am leading to is that all too often when you look at people you do not see people. Rather, *you see reflections of yourself.* Why is this true?

Once there was a cave man who did not know what he looked like. The way he gained a sense of his physical self was by looking in a pool of water, and if it was a clear pool of water it might reflect blue sky and he looked bluish. If it was a red, muddy pool he looked reddish; if it was rippled, he looked wrinkled; and if it was murky, he looked expressionless. Any pool of water could change his opinion of himself. Let us assume that we bring this cave man to our present time and take him to a circus with a side show of distorting mirrors. If he looked in the mirror he would believe that this is the way he really looked, and he might cry. If you look in this mirror, how do you react? You will laugh; but what if you called on someone and he said that you are incompetent and irresponsible—a complete distortion of what you really are? What would you do? Would you laugh, or might you cry?

Why can you laugh at the distorting mirror but not at the person who is critical of you? It is because, in our civilization, we have mirrors that tell us what we look like physically, and no distorting mirror can lie to us and have us believe it. We know what we look like. Yet, in this day and age we have not yet developed psychological mirrors of ourselves that tell us what we are like in terms of our inner personality. So you keep searching, and people are mirrors of you. They reflect back through their own positive or negative mind, and because you have never seen a clear image of yourself psychologically you tend to assume that the reflections you are getting are correct. This is even more likely if you tended to get positive reflections from your parents in childhood and therefore would like to assume that the reactions of others are a true reflection of yourself. Then, if you meet people who are hostile, you may continue to assume that the reactions of others are true reflections of yourself. Therefore, *just as your parents may have given you a positive self-image, others who may react negatively to you may take it away.*

More specifically, the self-image develops as the child expresses himself or herself to the human environment. The human environment reacts back to the child, creating in the child's mind an image of what he or she is like. Now, if you hope to change, you must understand the crucial relationship between your conscious and subconscious mind. It has been determined that your subconscious mind, where your potential is, does not think or make decisions. It has no eyes or ears and cannot tell what is going on. Your subconscious mind does only one thing, it follows what you consciously believe to be true. Therefore, your image of yourself within your conscious mind becomes the instructions to your subconscious mind, which carries out what you believe to be true.

Thus if you believe that you can lift this book from your hand, then your subconscious mind will carry out that positive thought. If you consciously believe that you cannot stretch out between two chairs, your head on one chair and your feet on the other with nothing supporting you underneath, then your subconscious will prove that it is true; and if you try, it will help you to fail. If you reverse these two beliefs, the subconscious mind will correspondingly change the way it reacts, and your results will change. Thus we come to one major challenge: If you can change your image of yourself you will automatically change the instructions to your subconscious mind. By changing the instructions to your subconscious mind you will begin to respond differently, and your new behavior will justify your new self-image.

As an example, a mackerel and a barracuda have been placed

in the same pool of water together. Now the barracuda loves mackerel, and as soon as it sees the fish it rapidly begins swimming for the attack. The only thing it does not know is that there is a thick piece of glass between it and that mackerel, and wham—right into the glass. It is in pain but does not know what has hit it, so it tries again; and again it has a bad experience. In fact, after a while the barracuda gets a headache just looking at the mackerel. Then they take the glass out of the pool of water and the mackerel swims by; but the barracuda keeps its distance, because it knows what it can or cannot do.

You have been conditioned in basically the same way. You get positive feedback that tells you what you can do, and you get negative feedback that tells you what you cannot do. If you assume that the reactions of others or the actual experiences you have are true reflections of your ability, *that* will become your self-image. What you assume to be true then becomes the instructions to your subconscious, determining your future behavior.

Self-image and IQ

An illustration of the dramatic relationship between the self-image and potential was presented in *The Los Angeles Times* on June 15, 1969, and relates the experience of a Dr. Harold M. Skeels with two girls born of mentally deficient mothers. One mother had an IQ of 35 and the other's was 46. Dr. Skeels had to realize that since these girls were born of such mentally deficient mothers they too would be mentally deficient, as it was assumed at this time that intelligence was inherited, physical, and genetic. For this reason these two girls could not be put into an orphanage, as the only purpose of an orphanage was for adoption proceedings, and it was assumed that these girls were not of adoptable material. The only place for them was a mental institution, so at the age of five days they were committed to a mental hospital for the rest of their lives.

Two years later the psychiatrist, making his rounds in the same hospital, came upon two girls who appeared to be normal in intelligence. Curious, he checked back and discovered that they were girls he had committed to the hospital previously. Could he have erred in placing them there? Investigating, he learned that when they were committed to the hospital they had been placed in an area with older girls whose physical ages were between nine and twelve and whose mental ages were between five and nine. These older girls probably didn't have enough toys, as they "adopted" the two girls as their babies. More specifically, they encouraged them to achieve and they loved them. The "mentally deficient" girls were now tested, found to have average intelligence, and sent out for adoption.

Dr. Skeels was so concerned that this might be merely an exceptional case that he went into an orphanage and took twenty-six children who were in the process of being adopted. Thirteen he allowed to be adopted and thirteen he held in that orphanage. One boy who was held in the orphanage dropped from an IQ of 103 to 49, because no matter how intelligent he was no one paid attention to him, no matter how personable he tried to be no one loved him, no matter how nice he tried to be no one cared. With a loss of encouragement to achieve and with a loss of love he lost over 50 percent of his IQ. The psychiatrist then concluded, "IQs are nothing more than a measure of the function of an individual at a given time. It's like a feather falling in a cyclone—what happens here, or there, along the lifespan, will affect it."

Thus we inherit our abilities genetically, but more importantly we inherit our environment. It is our environment that encourages or discourages our behavior. The way in which people react to our behavior thus determines our self-image. It is this image, then, that causes us to behave consistently from that point on, for as we see ourselves our subconscious accordingly responds. What experiences have you had in your past that have caused you to see yourself the way you do today? Why have you developed certain doubts that block you from operating effectively in important responsibilities that determine your success?

Your past experiences determine your self-image, and your self-image determines your attitudes toward your environment and yourself. Your attitudes then determine your habits—which in the final analysis determine your results. You can measure your self-image by examining your attitudes toward your environment and yourself, as your attitudes are an extension of your self-image.

If you have a negative attitude toward selling a certain product or selling to certain types of people, this is a reflection of a negative self-image. You might then want to ask yourself, "What experiences have I had to cause my image to be negative in this area, resulting in negative attitudes toward these responsibilities?" In turn, you can actually see the effect that your negative attitudes have on your behavior. These negative attitudes motivate you to develop negative habits or defense mechanisms that will cause you to avoid these responsibilities, but they will also block you from succeeding.

If you have difficulty determining your negative attitudes, then merely determine those responsibilities or activities that you tend to avoid. Do you avoid prospecting or closing? Do you avoid doing mechanical work around the house or spending time with the chil-

avoid giving presentations or writing proposals? What ιο avoid these responsibilities will represent your negative habits, which are the reflection of negative attitudes, which are the extension of a negative self-image, which has been caused by past experiences which you felt were a true reflection of your lack of ability.

In review: if, because of a bad experience, you feel you have a lack of ability, you will not want to fail again because that hurts your ego, your self-image, and your self-esteem. So you avoid the situation that makes you feel inadequate. Result: a negative self-image. The negative self-image causes you to have a negative attitude toward this aspect of your life, and, in order to avoid failure in these aspects of your life, you develop negative habits.

Again, the objective at this point is to determine where you negative self-image exists by examining your negative attitudes or negative habits. In this way you can make a chart listing in the first column your past experiences that have caused your image to be negative. Your negative image is then listed. In the third column you list your negative attitudes, then your negative habits, and the kind of negative results that occur. In the last column you should list the solutions that can help change your self-image.

Responsibility (such as)	Past Experiences	Positive or Negative				Solutions
		Self-image	Attitudes	Habits	Results	
Prospecting						
Follow-up						
Developing Rapport						
Discovering Needs						
Making Presentations						
Overcoming Objections						
Closing						
Financial						

Now determine one aspect of your self-image you should change at this time. Maybe it is an area that might be changed easily in order to get you into a positive momentum right now. Maybe it is an area that is crucial because it is the key to other aspects of your life, even though it might be difficult to change. Of all the aspects of your self-image there is one, though, that *must* be positive, and that is your ability to change. It is the most important ability you can have. So you can't drive a car, don't know how to close, and write clumsy letters. Yet *if you know how to change you can develop any ability that you need; but if you don't know how to change you will be doing tomorrow what you did yesterday.* Competent today, but if the world changes around you and you do not change with it, you may find yourself obsolete tomorrow.

When was the last time *you* changed? What is the last new skill or ability that you developed? How easy is it for you to change? If you realize you haven't been changing that often or that it has been a long time since you last changed, maybe you should change in some area of your life just for the sake of change. Maybe sign up for a class in a subject that allows you to develop another skill, take up a physical sport you've never tried—lose weight, stop smoking, start cycling, just to prove to yourself that you *can* change.

At this time decide what your goal is going to be—in terms of changing your self-image, attitudes, and habits—in preparation for twenty-four techniques for change.

VII

The Anatomy of Personality

If you could see the major parts of your personality as a total picture, you could better visualize the concepts that you have just studied. In this way the achievement of self-awareness and change will become an easier process.

There are specific aspects of your personality that are dynamic in the sense that they play a major role in determining your behavior and personal satisfaction. The process begins with your primary need to accept yourself. Since this need exists for everyone, we will therefore not include it in our discussion. Rather, we will be concerned about the needs that we must satisfy in order to gain self-acceptance.

The concern will not be with the need for money since this is only a steppingstone need. Admittedly, when we do not have it, we need it. Yet many salesmen who need money badly, when it comes time to close, will all too often be more concerned about being accepted and avoiding rejection. Therefore they do not close.

Again, as important a motivator as money might be, it is still a transitory need. If you have it, you are in a position to satisfy your major need. If you do not have it, it is often difficult to be concerned about any other need. Unfortunately, too many people are so concerned about financial security that they take very safe jobs in which they feel protected, even though they never become financially self-sufficient and never are able to move on to their next needs.

Values

Yet money can be a major motivator if it is your way of gauging how good you are. This brings us to the concept of values. Most people have some sort of value system, and at best it is a healthy one in the sense that it helps them develop their potential as well as the potential of those they work and live with. If the individual has not had success patterns, he may not have a strong value system in the sense of what "turns him on" or motivates him.

If he does not have a strong value system, then his basic need —to be comfortable—will usually be the major motivator. It will take very little money, achievement, or recognition to satisfy him because there is nothing that he is particularly after. He will feel that there is no value to be gained in striving.

Value refers to what you're after—what's important to you. The individual strives toward that which has value to him; if there is nothing of value, there is no need to strive. Another important word is *expectations*. If there *is* something you value, how much of it do you need before you will be satisfied? What are your expectations? Therefore, values determine what you need, and expectations determine how *much* you need. The first is qualitative, the second quantitative.

Need for Identity

Again, in order to gain a sense of your identity, a major need is to find out how effective you are, what do you have to achieve in order to discover that you are effective? If money is the way you keep score, you are not really looking at money as money but as an index of your effectiveness. Once you know what your major motivator is, you will know what your major fear, antineed, or demotivator is. If your major need is to discover how effective you are, then your major antineed will be the fear that you might discover that you are not as good as you would like to think you are.

This need for identity can be satisfied by other than financial success. Family, athletics, scholastic achievement, the arts, or management success are just a few of the ways we can achieve based on different value systems. The more this or any other need is satisfied, the less chance there will be that the fear will be triggered.

With the need for identity, this means that the more you discover how good you are, the less fearful you are of discovering weaknesses. The less sure you are of yourself the more upset you will become in confronting weaknesses. The more you realize how capable you are, the less reluctant you are to admit that you are not perfect. Again, expectations determine how much you must achieve within your value system before you can feel successful.

The higher the expectations, the greater the demand for achievement—and the greater the chances of frustration. If you base your expectations on the belief that you *should* do very well, then the drives may become very strong and should be relatively positive. If you want to find out how capable you can become but are afraid that you might not succeed—perhaps because you identified with parents who failed in some way—then you may be motivated primarily by fear. If you try to escape from your fears by succeeding, then your drives may often be defensive in nature. Thus the first need we have is for identity.

Need for Self-sufficiency

Another need is to be self-sufficient. Most people need money, not so much to discover what they are worth or to have a good life but to prove to themselves that they are independent. They need to prove that they do not need anyone and that they can operate on their own. This is another form of achievement with self-sufficiency as the primary value. Again, your expectations determine how self-sufficient you need to be before you can accept yourself.

Of course the antineed will be the fear of dependency on someone else, of being blocked from achieving your goals. So the more you believe you *can* become self-sufficient, the more you will strive with determination and without stress. The more you fear you might fail, the more you will react with anxiety and operate defensively.

Need to Control

The third need is to control or dominate. This is different from the need to be self-sufficient; as self-sufficiency requires that you operate on your own, while control requires succeeding through the positive or negative "manipulation" of others. This form of achievement, of course, is based on a different value system. The factor that determines how much the individual must control in order to feel successful is again "expectations."

Of course, the antineed is the fear of losing control or of being dominated by others. As with other needs and antineeds, the greater the fear the more difficult it is for the individual to reach a point where he can feel satisfied and comfortable. If the fear of being dominated is very strong, then the individual may have to control everyone in order to feel secure. Thus he himself is continually dominating—for defensive reasons—because he is trying to avoid the fear of losing control or being dominated by others.

Need to Be Accepted

The fourth need is to be accepted by others, and therefore the antineed is the fear of being rejected. The way we gain acceptance is by helping, liking, and pleasing others, and the way we avoid being rejected is by not doing anything that might displease or hurt people or cause them to feel we dislike them. This is the value system, and again the question is one of expectations. How much acceptance and love do we need before we can accept ourselves? How great is our fear of rejection, and how does fear influence our behavior?

If the individual does not have a strong value system, then he will not be able to handle anxiety. Why should he bother with anxiety if he does not want to go anywhere? Thus his major need is to be comfortable, and the antineed will be the fear of being uncomfortable or anxious. There are no expectations—just as there are no "hot buttons" or values. Therefore being comfortable is primary.

Other Needs and Conflict

Of course there are other needs, as well as other fears, but all have their roots in the ones we have discussed. As an example, sex is a major need, but as a physical need it belongs in the category of food and sleep. If sex becomes a way of discovering how good you are, of exercising control over others or of winning acceptance, sex itself is not the subject; ego is.

Again, your past experiences determine which needs will become the major influence in your life. If you grow up in poverty and your father never had a steady job, your major concern in life might be to avoid financial insecurity by finding a secure, set-salary job. If you were deprived of something that you really wanted in childhood, you may want to spend the rest of your life creating self-sufficiency so you can always do as you wish. If one of your parents in some way was a failure and you identify with him or her, then you may have a strong drive to prove that you are not the same. If you respected someone who was very domineering, then you may be motivated to control others. If you never were able to accept yourself unless you were first accepted by others—and some people rejected you in the past—then your major drive may be for acceptance. Again, the primary factor is not the experiences that you have had but your reactions to them. If you failed and experienced serious ego damage, then how do you react? It is not the ego damage which is the problem but the fact that you are motivated to avoid a task or challenge. If, instead, you are determined to conquer the fear of further ego damage by always being growth-oriented, then the initial failure experience may have been the best experience of your life.

Also, you will usually have more than one need. In fact, you will invariably have *all* the needs we have discussed. You may be motivated to control at work and to be accepted at home. Nevertheless, there is usually only one major need that primarily influences the individual's behavior. In some cases this becomes so extreme that the individual may seem obsessed.

While in some cases we may have to accept two major needs within a specific personality, the conflict may take another form. As an example, the individual may be motivated only by acceptance, but he may need it from both his work associates and his family. This may be healthy if he can achieve it; but if the need for both is very great, he may have difficulty being in the same place at the same time. It would almost be easier if, in this case, the individual did not particularly care about one or the other. Yet that will often create gaps within his life that can cause a number of other problems.

Once you have determined the major need that motivates you—as well as the corresponding fear, your value system, and the extent of your expectations, you must then determine how you react to these factors. Needs create desire to strive and fears cause anxiety and the wish to avoid. Now how do you react to desire and anxiety? The answer is determined by your defense mechanisms.

Needs and Defenses

Say your defense mechanism is warmth and sympathy. When you experience anxiety, you may have to bottle it up within yourself because your defense mechanisms will not allow for the expression of anxiety; such expression might threaten people, and that is incompatible with the empathetic individual.

This particular defense mechanism is usually used by people who need to be accepted and are afraid of being rejected. They try to eliminate threat by playing the "nice guy" game. "I am a nice guy. I wouldn't want to hurt you. Why would you want to hurt me?" In this way their defense mechanism helps them to gain acceptance and avoid rejection—but there are some liabilities.

First, the anxiety cannot easily be expressed for fear of offending someone; this might lead to rejection and further anxiety. Thus the warm, sympathetic defense causes anxiety to be turned inward—which leads to withdrawal. You may not be rejected, and you may even gain acceptance; but you may also suffer depression and inaction, resulting in a loss of personal achievement and success.

This can lead to a vicious circle. If a lack of achievement leads to rejection by those around you, then you will experience more anxiety and have a greater need to protect yourself. If possible, you will find a way to convert your anxiety into creative energy in order to capitalize on the anxiety, use the empathy persistently, or react in some positive way to your fear of rejection.

Therefore your needs usually determine the kind of defenses that you will develop. In the first example, the need to be accepted and the fear of being rejected motivate the individual to play the "nice guy" game. Yet it may not be that simple: if you fear rejection, you may develop the composure defense, in which the more you feel threatened the cooler you become until, just at the point you are ready for the funny farm, you appear so cool and relaxed that no one would ever suspect the seriousness of the problem. In this way you insulate yourself from emotional involvement and become insulated from rejection. You will also block yourself from the kind of achievement or acceptance that you need in order to be happy.

If the major need is to control, then the classic defense is aggressiveness with strength and confidence. Again, this does not mean that the individual *feels* aggressive and confident. In fact, the weaker he feels, the more aggressive and confident he may appear in order to better assure control. This defense mechanism allows him to express frustrations and anxiety readily. For this reason he may tend to react rather than withdraw and, while usually succeeding in achieving material goals, he may threaten people, which may lead to a breakdown in interpersonal relations, cause a loss of control, and result in frustration and anxiety. This vicious circle can all too often lead to a loss of material success, for it is difficult to achieve your goals when you have antagonized everyone.

Yet if the control-oriented individual knows that he needs the interpersonal relations in order to win, then he must at least add humor and friendliness to his defense. This will help him to use his anxiety constructively and should lead to greater material success and better interpersonal relationships.

The self-sufficient individual is more inner-oriented than people-oriented and therefore does not tend to play games. He will be more inclined to operate on his own, to be introspective and reactive in terms of expressing his emotions, and not to play games.

The self-sufficient individual is primarily motivated by the fear of depending on others. If someone interferes with his self-sufficiency he may become hostile, since he does not play games. He will usually express his anxiety outwardly. Since he tends to work on his own, he will usually use the anxiety to better achieve his goals.

The individual who is primarily motivated to discover how good he is will usually determine his potential by proving that he is self-sufficient or by controlling others. Expectations play a major role with this individual. If they are very high, he can experience considerable anxiety. The fear of discovering he is not as good as he would like to think he is will also be a major factor for anxiety. His success will be heavily dependent on how he reacts to the anxiety that might be caused by his high expectations or his fear of discovering weaknesses. Finally, if the individual has no major value system, then nothing will particularly motivate him except the basic need to be comfortable. In this situation the defense will usually be composure, so that if anxiety does begin to develop he will automatically protect himself by staying cool. The more uptight he becomes, the more composed he will appear.

With the composure defense he will not achieve, but this will not be particularly upsetting since he does not expect to succeed. But because he is working so hard to stay calm he may experience such problems as a lack of money as well as rejection by those who depend on him. This can result in the kind of anxiety which he is trying to avoid.

Goals as a Key to Needs

Which major need must you satisfy in order to gain self-acceptance? If you can tell me what you would do if you were wealthy, then I can tell you what your major motivator might be. If you would spend the rest of your life helping people, then your major motivator is probably the need for acceptance and the antineed is the fear of rejection. If you would spend the money gaining greater influence and position—whether through business, political, or social activity—then your major motivator is to control, with the antineed being the fear of losing control. If you would invest the money in areas that could help you to determine how much you could really accomplish, then your major need would be discovering your potential. The fear will be discovering that you are not as capable as you would like to think you are. If the need is to be self-sufficient, you will probably want an adventurous life where you are on your own and can be introspective. If the need is to be comfortable, you will want to have all your needs satisfied by others and to live in a nonachieving, vacation-type environment.

In the last example it is worth noting that while many people believe that the only way to enjoy life if you are rich is to be comfortable, a major part of our population would be very uncomfortable if all they did was relax. Tell the growth-oriented individual to relax and he becomes uptight. How do you react to the idea of just relaxing and being inactive for a major portion of time?

Now that you have at least a reasonable idea of what motivates you, the next question is what defense mechanisms you are using.

When people begin to threaten you, which of the following do you tend to become?

1.	aggressive	8.	humble
2.	composed	9.	humorous
3.	competent	10.	positive
4.	concerned	11.	sincere
5.	confident	12.	strong
6.	enthusiastic	13.	sympathetic
7.	friendly	14.	warm

Again, the combination of defenses used determines whether you turn the anxiety inward or outward. If you turn the anxiety outward, your defense also determines how you convert the anxiety outward and therefore the kinds of results you will gain. If the results satisfy your needs and disarm your fears, then you will be in a positive cycle. If your need is not satisfied or your fear is triggered, or both, then a negative cycle will be created. If this continues, you may reach the danger zone of your anxiety level, which may cause you to withdraw. Equally, if you continue to withdraw, you may reach the point where you explode emotionally or overreact. What kinds of cycles do you find yourself experiencing?

_____

_____

_____

The way you tend to react determines the kind of experiences you are going to have, both positive and negative. The experiences that you have will determine your image, both positive and negative, as well as your attitudes and habits. As you continue to have the same kinds of experiences, your positive and negative self-image becomes stronger and in this way assures that your behavior will continue unchanged, regardless of whether it benefits you or hurts you.

Your ability to recognize the interaction of your needs and fears, your defense mechanisms, the expression of your positive and negative emotions, the kinds of results you experience, the cycles that result, and the development of your self-image, attitudes, and habits will enable you to see a total picture that should prepare you for the next process, which is to change. To know yourself is the first objective, but you should capitalize on your self-awareness by taking action.

Where should you begin? Should you disengage the fears, modify the defenses, more constructively channel the anxiety, change your self-image, attitudes, or habits, improve the results, or change the cycles? I suggest you work on all these areas for the greatest improvement in total effectiveness.

VIII

Twelve Goal-achieving Techniques

Before reading this chapter, you should first write down your goals. You may want to set a goal based on the material in the first part of this text, such as, "I would like to convert anxiety into creative energy," or "I would like to rebound with empathy whenever anyone challenges me." Maybe you are more concerned about a personal goal such as "I would like to stop smoking," or a financial goal such as "I would like to make $25,000 in the next twelve months," or a physical goal such as "I would like to jog a mile per day." Do not go any further until you decide what your goal is at this time, so that these twenty-four techniques will be more meaningful because they can be applied immediately.

Incidentally, when you write down your goals, do you put them in the future or present tense? Goals are usually written in the future tense, such as, "I am going . . . , I shall . . . , I will . . . , I expect to. . . . " If you are going to change, you must first understand that your subconscious mind does not think in the future. It only follows what you consciously believe to be true right now. You know that when you describe yourself, you do so in the present. You might say, "I am a good prospector but I have difficulty closing." This is in the present tense, and your subconscious, because it thinks in the present, follows these instructions and determines your behavior.

1. Positive Affirmation

For this reason your first technique is called positive affirmation, which means affirming to yourself *in the present tense* who you are right now. This means that you would state, "I enjoy converting anxiety into creative energy," or "I never see failure as failure but only that which I have to go through to succeed." This technique can create very rapid change. As an example, I once helped a woman stop smoking in thirty seconds. She had always been saying to herself, "I am going to stop smoking. I am going to, I really am going to." What did her subconscious say? "O.K., tell me when, because obviously you are not ready yet." "I am going to" is not the way to set goals. At this point she said, "I am a nonsmoker," *and she never smoked again.*

If you set a financial goal by stating, "I am going to make $25,000 in the next twelve months if everything goes well and I have a few lucky breaks. At least I hope that I can do it," what kind of success can you expect? Imagine if you were a subject in a hypnosis show and the hypnotist said to you, "You are going to be as straight as a board. I mean, if everything goes O.K. and we have a few lucky breaks—that's probably a poor term to use—but if everything goes O.K., I think that you might possibly be able to. . . . " Now what kind of a chance will the hypnotist have in a situation like this? You would not believe him. *Yet that is how your subconscious reacts when you use such words as* think, maybe, hope, going to, will, would, possibly; *it does not believe you.* It only follows what you believe to be true, in the present tense and in a definite form. For this reason take your goal that you have written down and phrase it as a *positive affirmation.*

As an example, one insurance salesman who wanted to make $25,000 never got over $12,000 until he wrote a sign on his office door that said "$25,000." Every time he came into his office, closed the door, and sat down, he would look up and see the $25,000 figure, and it told him one thing: the only way you are going to make it is to pick up the telephone and start making calls. It was a constant reminder of who he was and what he had to do to succeed.

Positive affirmations can have a dramatic result for you. Nevertheless, they might not work if you do not believe them. For this reason your second technique should help to make your positive affirmation more effective.

2. Descriptive Technique

In this technique you describe the kind of person you want to be. Often the positive affirmation does not work because you really don't know what you're striving toward. You need a clear vision of what you're after. The better you describe the route to your goal, the greater your chance of believing the positive affirmation and behaving accordingly. Now take two sheets of paper. On the first sheet, describe in detail the kind of life-style that you wish to have in the future, whether one year from now or five years from now. On the second sheet, describe in detail the daily schedule that will create the kind of success that will allow you to have that kind of life-style. In this way you will better sense the relationship between your present activity and future results, as well as better sensing the kind of person you have to be today in order to achieve your objectives.

Another way of using the descriptive technique is more dramatic. First, how much money do you want to make in the next twelve months? As an example, if your goal is $25,000, that would be $500 per week. Now imagine that you have hired someone to sell your product and you are going to pay him $500 per week out of your own pocket. What would you expect him to do each day? How many calls would you expect him to make? How many appointments would you expect him to have in advance? How many times would you expect him to close before he would give up? Many salesmen become particularly upset when they begin to realize that they are not doing per day what they would expect *someone else* to do for the kind of money that they would like to achieve. If you are not doing per day what you would expect someone else to do for that amount of money, then what do you think is the problem?

3. Incentive Technique

Another reason people have difficulty achieving their goals is that they are not convinced it is important to achieve them. It is similar to the case of the salesman who is called in by his manager to discuss his goals for the year and who thinks to himself, "I wonder what he wants to hear?" The salesman then goes on to role play his answer by discussing goals that he feels will satisfy his manager. Yet we have a tendency to do the same thing with ourselves. We have a tendency to set those goals that we think we *should* set, even though sometimes we really do not plan on achieving them. You might *think* you want to achieve the goal and thus make some initial efforts toward it, but deep inside yourself you do not really plan on persevering until you reach it. You have not really sold yourself on the need to achieve the goal. For this reason you should apply the third technique, the incentive technique.

Whenever you are selling someone, you should do more than just tell him the features of your product. You should also list the benefits to be derived from buying your product. In the same way you should make a list of the benefits to be derived from achieving your goal.

As an example, if your goal is to convert anxiety into creative energy, what are the benefits to be derived from achieving this goal? First, you will be more consistently successful. You will also create a more positive impact on others. Further, you will feel better, and fourth, you will be *more* successful; and isn't that what you are after? There are four major benefits to be derived from converting anxiety into creative energy; and the more you are sold on the importance of achieving the goal, the greater the chances that you will persevere until you have succeeded.

4. Fear Technique

If the incentive technique does not assure your success, use the fear technique. I do not recommend negative motivation, but if the first three techniques do not work, then maybe you need something that might create enough anxiety to force you to begin. The fear technique requires that you make a list of all the negative consequences of your failure to achieve your goal.

Again, if your goal is to convert anxiety into creative energy, what disadvantages will you face if you do not achieve the goal? First, you will find yourself in peaks and valleys rather than consistent success. Further, you will tend to make a negative impact on others because you will all too often be depressed or irritable. Third, you will not feel very good inside. You may experience hypertension and migraine headaches as well as trouble sleeping at night, and you will not be as successful as you should be. In fact, you may fail. Again, you should *not* remind yourself of such negatives unless the positive techniques are not working.

5. Total Commitment

The fifth technique is total commitment. Before we discuss its importance, you might ask yourself why people have so much difficulty making a total commitment. It is because they are afraid to fail. If you make a total commitment and you fail, how much do you fail by? You fail totally, and that can really hurt. That is why I find that so many people are willing to try almost anything a *little* bit; for if you do something a little bit and fail, how much can you fail by? Yet you know that the important goals in life are not achieved by trying just a little bit. They require *total commitment*.

It is similar to the way you get a plane off the ground. It requires 100 percent throttle; but once you are in the air, you can cruise at 50 or 60 percent throttle. Yet many people try to get off the ground with 50 percent effort, and they find themselves crashing into trees because *you do not get off the ground with half an effort*.

I once had a student tell me in the early part of a seminar that the reason he was taking my class was to discover why he was not doing the things that would assure his success. Later on in the seminar I used hypnosis, and placing him in a hypnotic state I asked him, "What is your major obstacle at this time?" After the session he told me that while in the hypnotic state these words started coming to him: "The reason I am not doing the things that will guarantee my success is that if I do them and fail then it means that I'm the failure." Is it possible that there are times when you are reluctant to do those things that will assure your success for fear that if you do what you should be doing and still fail, it will mean that you are the failure?

As an example, there is the story of the chicken and the pig who were walking down the street one day and came upon a restaurant with a sign saying, "Ham and Eggs, 79¢." The chicken was really proud about those eggs and she began strutting back and forth claiming, "What would breakfast be without eggs? Eggs and breakfast are synonymous," and she was going on and on until finally the pig interrupted her and said, "Yes, you are absolutely right. But with me, it is a total commitment." That is the challenge to you, to be able to make that total commitment.

The power of this technique is illustrated by the laser beam, which can cut through almost anything. Yet a laser beam consists only of light, the same light that surrounds you each day. The only difference is that the light energy in a laser beam is concentrated, and that creates the power. You are like light energy. You have a tremendous power within you, but your energy and ability must be concentrated. You cannot allow fear or stress to dilute or misdirect the power within you. A total commitment to your objectives can bring your strengths together into just such a force.

6. Vivid Imagination

Your sixth technique is vivid imagination. While you may have difficulty believing this, it is a fact that your subconscious mind cannot tell the difference between a real and an imagined fact. It only follows what you consciously believe to be true, whether real or assumed. Therefore, if you wish to attain a goal that you have never achieved before, you can do so because *imagining* that you *have* achieved the goal will cause your subconscious mind to believe it and to respond accordingly.

A most dramatic example of vivid imagination occurred in the 1968 Olympics, with Dick Fosbury trying for the high jump. The bar was set at 7 feet, 4¼ inches. This meant that Fosbury had to jump a foot and a half over the top of his head. Fosbury's technique was that when he reached the bar, he would turn around and jump backward into the air.

That Sunday afternoon, he had his fists clenched, and he was rocking back and forth. Observers wondered if he was ever going to try, as it seemed he was going to spend the entire day just rocking back and forth. As he explained afterwards, he was trying to concentrate until he could finally see himself running step by step, imagine himself turning backwards and leaping into the air, visualize himself clearing the bar with a couple of inches to spare, and feel himself landing safely. At the point at which he could imagine himself doing it, the physical part was easy. On his first try he did jump a foot and a half over the top of his head, backwards, and the lowest part of his body was never within 2 inches of that bar.

You have the same ability to imagine yourself succeeding before you try. In fact, you have probably used this technique of vivid imagination—as when you applied for your present job. Maybe you have imagined, as you drove to the interview, the manager asking you why you felt you would be qualified to sell his particular product. While you may not have felt completely sure of yourself, you could visualize yourself answering the question with confidence. The better you imagined yourself answering it, the more confident you felt— as your subconscious began to believe that is was true and helped you to respond accordingly.

From this day on, I would like you to imagine yourself succeeding before you try. Before you make that prospecting call, that presentation, or try to close, first see yourself succeeding. Whenever you are trying something where you are not yet confident, first imagine yourself succeeding. You will find your subconscious responding in such a way that you will notice an immediate improvement in your effectiveness. By reprogramming your self-image, you change your results. If the technique does not help you, then try imagining why you are not succeeding.

7.   Honesty Technique

If the first six techniques do not work, it is possible that your defense mechanisms are too strong; and while they are protecting you, they may also be blocking you from your objectives.

Your seventh technique is the honesty technique in which, merely by being honest with yourself and determining what your defense mechanism is, you are able to accept the responsibility that you have to yourself to strive forward. We have already discussed in detail the nature of defense mechanisms and their value as well as the problem they can create when they block you. For this reason determine the kind of game you are playing that might be blocking you from success and the kind of game you should start playing that, while giving you a sense of protection, will also help you to achieve. As an example, if your present defense is to protect yourself by procrastinating, then you may not fail today, but neither will you succeed. If you were to find someone who would prospect with you, this would be a defense, since you are avoiding failure by depending on someone else. Yet if it helps you to achieve, then it is much healthier than your present defense mechanism of avoidance.

8. Obstacle Technique

Often the difficulty in achieving goals is not so much a lack of ability in striving toward the goals as it is a problem of confronting obstacles that often block us. If you do not know what the obstacles in your path are, it is understandable that you may become frustrated in the process of trying to achieve the goal. Many people who read self-improvement books are often frustrated because the books tell them to think positively and believe in themselves, and for this reason they have high expectations. Nevertheless, something seems to block them from reaching those high expectations, even though they try. Something is blocking them which causes them to short-circuit on the way. Often it is because they are afraid of failure or because they may have difficulty handling the anxiety as part of the process of trying. For this reason, if the first techniques do not work, it invariably means there is an obstacle blocking you from success and you should determine what it might be.

There are two basic types of obstacles you can confront. One is a negative self-image and the other is the fear of failure or rejection. If you were to have difficulty achieving a particular goal, what might be the cause? The classic problem of the fear of failure in selling occurs with the well-educated individual, particularly when he is technically oriented. A specific example might be an engineer who has been in the same job for twenty years.

If the aerospace industry in which he works experiences an economic slump, he may find himself laid off. He begins to realize that the job security he had was an illusion and that what he should be doing is getting into a job that allows him to become financially self-sufficient. After six months of discouragement in which his résumés go unanswered, he decides to become a salesman. In the training program he has difficulty grasping the material as rapidly as some of the trainees who lack his educational background or business experience. His first day on the job, he makes twenty-five calls and twenty-five people turn him down. Now he finds himself becoming defensive rather than enthusiastically decisive. His self-image is becoming damaged by these negative experiences, and he finds himself becoming more concerned about protecting what he has left than taking chances and trying to expand his self-image. He is afraid of failure and rejection.

In contrast, take the high school dropout who is working in a retail store for $120 per week and wants to buy a new sports car and live in a better apartment. For these reasons he goes into a straight commission sales position and immediately begins making $160 per week, just what he needs to buy the things that he is after. His manager is impressed with his ability to become productive immediately and feels that if he were better educated he might be even more successful. The manager sends him to special sales programs, and within a matter of weeks he is twice as effective—which means that he can make the same amount of money in half the time. Rather than double his income he takes up golf. He is able to handle failure and rejection and thus quickly reaches the stage of what he believes he is worth. At that particular point he levels off, and unless his image is upgraded, he will not go any further. His problem is a negative self-image.

It is like an air-conditioner thermostat that might be set for 70 degrees. Whenever it reaches 71 degrees, the machine goes on and brings the temperature to 69 degrees. At what income level do you turn yourself on? What experiences have you had that cause you to see yourself at your present level but that might block you from greater success?

Which problem do you feel you are experiencing at this time—fear of failure or a negative self-image? Of course, there are people who have both problems to some degree and others who have neither problem and are fully capitalizing on their potential and reaching significant levels of success. Yet your potential is so great that most people have difficulty comprehending how capable they really are and for this reason do not fully capitalize on their inner abilities. While you may have a very positive self-image compared to most people, illustrated by your success, it may be negative compared to your actual ability.

While we have been discussing these two problems that people can experience—fear of failure and negative self-image—it should be realized that both these problems have the same common roots. In a very basic sense there is only one problem that people can experience. What might that be? First let's examine the two obstacles, one at a time, to trace their common roots. Why are people afraid of failure? It is not so much the failure that people are afraid of but the rejection which might follow. People are afraid of rejection because they need to be accepted by others before they can accept themselves. It is this tremendous need for acceptance from others which causes people to be oversensitive to the reactions of others.

In the same respect, what causes us to develop a negative self-image? We have a need to find out who we are in order to decide if we can accept ourselves. For this reason we are very concerned about the opinions of others, as people are mirrors that reflect an image of who we are. Since we are primarily dependent on the reactions of others for a sense of who we are, we tend to be oversensitive to the reactions of others. There is the problem—oversensitivity to the reactions of others.

Being sensitive to the reactions of others is healthy, for their reactions give you a sense of yourself; but when you become oversensitive it may cause you to become defensive and to begin avoiding your goals. It is like ice which can be refreshing in your drink—but how does ice become hot ice? When it becomes so cold that you cannot touch it. It is the same with sensitivity toward people. To be sensitive to others is healthy, and to be liked by others is refreshing; but when you are so sensitive to the reactions of others that failure and rejection can cause a negative self-image and ego damage, then your sensitivity has become oversensitivity.

For this reason you must realize that there are three objectives that you can have with people. The first objective is to avoid rejection, which is a particularly negative situation. The second objective is to strive to be accepted by others. This can be dangerous because you are depending on other people, but at least you are striving; and if you achieve the acceptance of others, you may be able to grow through it. The primary objective is to find your acceptance within yourself. In this way you are able to strive toward those goals that fulfill your potential and satisfy your needs. You no longer require the reactions of others except as the feedback that you need in order to make changes in your course. Where are you? Are you striving to avoid rejection, striving to gain acceptance from others, or striving to fulfill your own potential? Possibly you are doing all three, depending on whom you are with, under what circumstances, and in what position.

9. Strength Bombardment

In preparation for your ninth technique, we find that most people are too aware of their weaknesses. One of the main criticisms of sensitivity training programs is that they all too often concentrate on everything that is wrong with the individual, and the more aware he becomes of his weaknesses the less confidence he has in himself. While it is helpful to be aware of shortcomings in order to correct them, it is a fact that if you are aware of more than one at a time you start to become discouraged and confused as to where to begin. Correspondingly, the more aware you are of your strengths, the more expansive you start to feel, and the more confidence you will gain to overcome any shortcomings you might have. For this reason, your ninth technique is referred to as "strength bombardment."

I would like you at this time to make a list of all your strengths. If you have difficulty getting beyond a few, then it indicates that you do not think well enough of yourself.

Part of this technique requires that you go back into your past and make a list of previous successes. Regardless of how small the success may have been—whether in sports, school, the family, the community, or with your peers—list the experience and determine what you did that caused it to be a success. Why did you react positively? Again, the more you recognize your strengths, the more positive you will feel about making new efforts for greater levels of success. In expanding your list, also ask at least two other people what strengths they feel you have.

From another perspective, you will find that as you list your strengths you will also be discovering what kind of image you have of yourself, what motivates and demotivates you, and where you will tend to succeed or fail with people. As an example, what do you learn about someone who says, "My strengths are that I like people, people like me, I enjoy helping people, I am good at developing rapport and discovering what people's needs are, and I enjoy helping people satisfy their needs or solve their problems." This indicates a good strength orientation because the individual is able to make an extensive list. Further, it indicates that his major motivator is to be accepted by people, and therefore he has developed strengths in this area. These allow him to have a positive self-image in developing relationships with people. In turn, it indicates that he may have a fear of rejection. This fear may culminate in a negative self-image when it comes to being decisive with others. For this reason people will tend to feel that he is concerned about them, but they will tend to feel also that he is indecisive.

What does it indicate if, as you list your strengths, you make such statements as, "I enjoy taking command of situations. I love the challenge of persuading people to my way of thinking and I am very action-oriented. I like to get results, particularly in competitive situations." This indicates that your major motivator is to control and your major demotivator is the fear of being controlled or being dependent on someone else. It also indicates that you have a positive self-image when it comes to being aggressive, but you probably have a negative self-image when it comes to being sympathetic with people. You will find that by listing your strengths, you will be telling yourself a great deal about many important aspects of your own personality and behavior.

10. Positive Thinking

In preparation for your next technique, I am sure you will accept the fact that there will always be negative and positive aspects throughout your life. If you tend to be oriented to the negative aspects, then you will feel justified in avoiding. If you do try, you will tend to do so with caution. In hesitancy there is a lack of strength, with failure too often following. Invariably when you do fail you determine why you have failed and thus convince yourself that you should not try again.

With the same thought in mind you can develop the important ability to find the advantage in every difficult situation. This is the technique of positive thinking, in which you always try to determine how an idea or a situation can benefit you, even when there might be negative aspects to it.

It is you who decide what thoughts will play in your mind, and these thoughts are the instructions to your subconscious potential. These thoughts tell your mind how to respond. If you think you cannot, then you will not try; and if you think you may not be able to, you will move cautiously. If you believe that you *can*, then you will move more aggressively; and if you believe that you *will*, you will become enthusiastically decisive. What you think about today will often be what you will experience tomorrow. Think *positive*.

11. Challenge Thinking

Your eleventh technique is challenge thinking. I can put people into two major categories: people who see obstacles as obstacles and people who see obstacles as their only opportunity to prove how good they can be. How do you find out how capable you can be? How do you test and fulfill your potential? By testing yourself. The problem with most people is that they view obstacles only as threats to their egos causing tension and demotivation. The successful individual sees an obstacle as his only opportunity to find out how good he can be, thus generating the kind of determination that motivates him to strive forward. If a customer cancels an order or you have not had any sales for a lengthy period of time, how do you react? If you see these problems as a threat to your ego, you will become defensive and avoid facing your problems; but if you realize that the more difficult the situation is, the greater your chances of proving your capability, you will accept the challenge and do battle.

A good example of challenge thinking is that of a seven-year-old boy who was in a fire so serious that it burned his companion to death. His legs were so badly burned that the doctors explained to him that he would never be able to walk again, and that if he tried to walk he would only experience extreme pain. For some reason he did not believe the doctors, and after weeks his legs finally healed enough for him to be on crutches. The first day he took off the crutches, he collapsed. Every time he tried to walk he experienced the kind of pain the doctors predicted, but for some reason he persisted. As the weeks went by, he learned to walk again, changing the views of physical therapists on this kind of muscle injury. Yet he was not satisfied, because he wanted to be as strong as other kids. For this reason he went out in the fields and ran miles every day; and in his effort to be as good as average, Glen Cunningham went on to set the world's record for the mile.

The problem for too many people is that they have never really failed; they have no scar tissue on their egos. How do you react to threatening or challenging situations, obstacles, or problems? How do you react when you find irritants within yourself? When an oyster finds a grain of sand within its shell, it converts it into pearl. What do you do when you find irritants within yourself that are cutting your insides? Do you withdraw in order to avoid the problem or do you convert these irritants into pearls of new strength? The tougher the situation, the greater the opportunity to develop new abilities and strengths.

12.   Obstacle Conversion

Your twelfth technique is obstacle conversion—converting obstacles into strengths. In this particular technique you transform the obstacle, whatever it might be, into a challenging thought— eliminating the obstacle! As an example, the major obstacle that people confront is the fear of rejection. Now how can you take that negative thought, "I'm afraid of rejection," and convert it to a positive thought? One example: "I'm inspired by the challenge of gaining acceptance." Another: "I reject rejection."

If your major obstacle is a negative self-image, in the sense that you believe you have achieved as much as you feel you are capable of, then convert that negative thought into a challenging thought that can resolve the problem: "I enjoy proving that I can continue to grow and reach new levels of achievement." The most challenging obstacle that people confront is, "I am oversensitive to the reactions of others." For this reason the most important thought that you can have, in terms of converting obstacles into strengths, is, "Whenever I find myself overreacting to the feelings of others, I know this means I have gone beyond my inner confidence and I need to force myself into new success patterns within this area of uncertainty." Specifically, "Oversensitivity to the reactions of others tells me I have not yet attained what I should." Another approach from the first chapter is "I enjoy the negative reactions of others because it is the feedback I need in order to make changes in my course."

Take the thoughts that are appropriate for you, whether they are mine or thoughts you have developed for yourself, and put them on index cards, on your mirror, or on your desk as constant reminders of what you are striving toward.

IX

Twelve More Goal-achieving Techniques

13. Acceptance Span

Your thirteenth technique is called "acceptance span," or, "How much can you believe?" To capitalize on this technique first requires some thought regarding the challenge of change. Within every block or doubt that you may have there is a degree of negative conditioning. This negative conditioning is based on the intensity of each negative experience you may have had that led to this block or doubt—as well as to the extent to which you assumed that these negative experiences were a true reflection of your lack of ability.

At this time I give you three words that can eliminate any negative conditioning, blocks, or fears that you may ever experience in life. The first word is *change*. That is what this book is about: that you are worthy of new levels of success and therefore you need to change; that you have the ability to change and should not be afraid of failure in the process of changing. It is so important that you be able to change that it is comparatively unimportant how much you change—as long as you begin to change. That is our second word, to *begin*. In order to begin, you must find something that you can believe, and therefore the third word is *believe*.

I once worked with a salesman who was having difficulty getting started. I asked him how many calls he was making per day, and he said his goal per day was twenty cold calls. I asked him how many he was making. None, he said. I asked him what the problem was, and he told me he just could not see himself being rejected twenty times in a single day. I then asked him if he could make fifteen calls per day, and he said, "No, that would be too many." Could he make ten calls? "That also would be too many." I asked him if he could make five calls per day, and he said, "Five phone calls. That would be hardly anything." Since five seemed to be no problem to him, I asked him to agree to make at least five calls per day. He began making the five calls, and within a few weeks he was making fifteen and twenty calls per day. With this technique of finding something he could believe in order to begin to change, he succeeded.

If you cannot handle enough failure to succeed, how much failure *can* you handle? If you stay depressed too long, could you at least begin reacting somewhat sooner? If you tend to be empathetic and have difficulty being persistent, how much more persistent could you at least be? If you cannot jog a mile per day, could you at least walk and jog a mile per day? Could you at least walk down to the corner and back again? How much would you believe? Remember, a journey of a thousand miles begins with a single step. Just find something you can believe in order to begin to change.

14. Tailored Technique

The fourteenth technique is the tailored technique, in which you discover ideas and methods that are tailored to your personality and make the process of striving a more comfortable one. If you are having difficulty prospecting or closing, you should brainstorm with associates or your boss, a technique that can increase your chances of success with a minimum of irritation. If you want to stop smoking, you should carry a candy that you like with you so that when you want a cigarette you take a piece of candy instead. If you tend to get depressed easily, you should find something that you enjoy doing that could help you become more active, so that you can eliminate the anxiety and get back to achieving.

If you have difficulty jogging a mile per day, then try running in a grassy area where there is less pressure on your legs. Or, try running with a companion so that you have a sense of competition as well as somebody else to think about besides yourself. In addition, try running in one large circle rather than around the same area again and again, so you reduce monotony as well as the temptation to stop each time you get back to where you started. Further, think of something other than running, and you will often be surprised to find yourself finishing your workout without really having been irritated by the effort.

With regard to the goal that you are presently striving toward—start developing techniques that can make it more comfortable for you to achieve that goal. Often success comes not so much from working harder but from working smarter.

15. Self-competition

Your next mind-conditioning technique is self-competition. The classic problem of being oversensitive to the reactions of others often takes the form of comparing yourself with others. If you compare yourself with people who have attained greater success than you, you will begin to feel inadequate and frustrated, which can reduce your effectiveness. If you compare yourself with people who are not doing as well as you, you might feel justified when you fail. The day has to come when you stop comparing yourself with others and begin to set your own standards—by competing with yourself!

Competition is good, but don't lose sight of your primary objective: to strive toward those goals that satisfy *your* needs and fulfill *your* potential. Otherwise you may find yourself distracted from the goals you should be achieving and veer toward goals that are more related to the needs, values, and potential of others. Further, your objective is to continuously strive to develop your acceptance within yourself, and this is better achieved through self-competition, which is inner-oriented, than through competition with others, which is outer-oriented.

How many more calls can you make this week versus last week? How much more in commissions can you earn this month versus last month? How many more miles can you jog this year versus last year? By competing with yourself, you create a positive momentum that leads to greater personal effectiveness.

16. Commitment to Others

Your sixteenth technique is commitment to others. This is one of the strongest techniques because it reverses the fear of rejection and causes this fear to literally force you into success. You tend to avoid doing what you should be doing because you are afraid that changing will cause more anxiety than not changing. For this reason you must find some way to cause more anxiety if you do *not* change. If you commit yourself to someone and fail in this commitment, you might be rejected. The rejection—or the thought of being rejected—will cause anxiety. If the possibility of being rejected causes more anxiety than actually making the change, then you will find it easier to do it than to avoid it.

In the past you changed because people forced you into it. They caused you more anxiety if you did not change, making it more comfortable to change than to avoid change. All too often your problem today is that there is no one forcing you into change. You can re-create the same situation by committing yourself to other people. It may be uncomfortable to have people hassle you into achievement, but you know that it is the way to develop the skills and abilities that create greater success and personal satisfaction.

Decide what you should be doing at this time within your business, the physical area of your life, your family, and your personal life. If you are having difficulty achieving your goals within these areas of your life, then make commitments to people who know you well and have an interest in your success.

17. Leadership

Leadership is your next technique. Interestingly, we often achieve only because we are setting standards for others. There are three benefits to be gained from trying to help other people to achieve —particularly in areas that coincide with your own interest—such as jogging a mile a day, prospecting at least an hour per day, continuing your education, or, within the family, helping your children develop new skills. By assisting someone else toward goals within your areas of interest, you upgrade your own self-image, for you see yourself in a position of leadership. Further, telling someone what *he* should be doing reinforces within your own mind the efforts you should be making. The third benefit is that if the other individual succeeds by following your advice, it may convince you all the more that you can also achieve the same objectives.

If it's a physical goal you can't manage, convince someone else that he should be working out with you each day; by joining you, he'll force you into it. Having difficulty prospecting an hour per day? Find someone who is not doing it and show him how to succeed. By demonstrating to someone else how to do it, you will also have to do it. If you are not spending as much time with your children as you should, ask one of your neighbors who has the same problem to join you on the weekend for some group activities. If you just can't get started in some personal development program, such as a course you should be taking, persuade someone else that he should also take it; then you have no choice but to begin.

18. Competition

Your eighteenth technique is competition. While it is preferable to compete with yourself and set your own standards, you should start competing with other people if the self-competition does not work. As an example, it is often better as a salesman to concentrate not on the actual sales but on the activities that create sales. If you were to make a list of all the activities that determine the success of a salesman—such as sending out direct mail, prospecting, making appointments, and giving presentations—and put a value on each one of these activities, you would then have a formula for success. You will now discover that you can be more successful if you would just concentrate on these activities. For instance, you might give yourself one point for each direct mail piece sent out, five points for each prospecting call, ten points for each appointment, fifteen points for each proposal, and twenty-five points for each presentation. Then compete with one of your associates on how many points can be scored each week. The competition can take your mind off yourself, help you to realize that other people are experiencing the same problem, and, most important of all, force you to achieve.

19. Acting As If

Before discussing the nineteenth technique, you must realize that if the first eighteen techniques have not worked it is probably because you just cannot see yourself as the kind of person you would like to be. If so, then use the nineteenth technique—fake it. This technique is formally referred to as "acting as if," in which you role play the situation in order to get started. You may not like the idea of playing games or role playing, but many of your present personality characteristics have developed in just that way.

Think back to childhood when you found yourself threatened by someone or you wanted to gain an objective but felt unsure of yourself. Imagine a fourteen-year-old boy calling a girl for his first date and what would happen if he projected the way he actually felt. With a great deal of hesitancy he might begin by saying, "This is . . . John Smith. I was wondering if you might be interested . . . if you might be interested . . . in going to the junior . . . whatever it is . . . my mother told me to call you up and ask if . . . you wouldn't want to go with me, would you?".

Another boy might call up and act as if he were confident and sure of himself; "This is John Smith. I think you'd enjoy going with me to the dance this Saturday night. May I pick you up at seven o'clock or seven-thirty?" If she responds positively, he begins to believe that he is cool and confident.

Tell me how you want to feel, and I can tell you how to feel that way. Do you want to feel confident, humorous, enthusiastic, poised, or friendly? If you want to feel confident, all you have to do is get people to treat you as an authority. Now how can you get people to treat you as an authority if you do not feel confident? Act like an authority. Fake it. The telephone company recommends it. They will talk to you about the importance of being friendly when using the telephone and tell you that if you are serious and intense you cannot expect people to be receptive to you. If you do not feel friendly, smile anyway. You may not feel like smiling, but if you force yourself you will find that you will also be speaking in a friendlier way. Now people will start becoming more responsive to you, and this will help you to feel friendlier.

Don't be afraid to fake it. You used the same technique in childhood to develop the characteristics that apply to your personality today. When you were born, you had the potential to be the kind of personality that you are today. Gradually you projected certain characteristics, gained favorable response, and began to see yourself as that type of individual. And you *became* that individual. On the other hand, there may have been certain characteristics, such as humor, that you tried, but you failed to get the feedback you expected or wanted. You therefore did not try again for fear of failing again. So, assuming that this particular characteristic was not one of your strengths, you put it back on the shelf and left it there.

Yet all possible characteristics of personality were within you at birth and are within you now. All you have to do is develop them. If you have tried and failed, you can still try again. All you have to do is be willing to *act as if* as well as be willing to fail in the process of developing new strengths. In this way you can build a personality anybody can identify with. Decide at this time what characteristics could help you become more effective, and start faking it. Your success in the development of new personality characteristics can have a positive effect on the achievement of your goals in other areas of your life.

To illustrate: if you make believe you are confident and people begin to treat you as though you are, you will not only strengthen your impact on others but also increase your ability to release anxiety. This is because people who meet frustration with confidence are usually not challenged. Thus by developing this quality you eliminate anxiety, gain a greater position of authority and therefore achieve more. If you keep your empathy you will not antagonize people but actually win them to you.

20. Exaggeration

Your twentieth technique is exaggeration. If you are having difficulty achieving a particular objective such as developing a new personality characteristic, exaggerate it! Do this in front of the mirror in the morning, and exaggerate the projection of confidence. You might try exaggerating this characteristic on a tape recorder or in a role-playing situation.

Then, when you try it *without* exaggerating, it will be easier for you to achieve it in a more balanced way! If you are having difficulty prospecting, then you should take a whole day and marathon prospect. In this way you will discover how many calls you can make in a single day—and come to realize that such an effort is possible and that twenty prospecting calls are no longer difficult.

21. GOYA

If the first twenty techniques do not help you to succeed, then before moving on to the twenty-first technique we should first discuss the reasons for your difficulty in becoming positively motivated. What is the first thing you do whenever you try to succeed? You start to think—but what do you think of? Of what you are going to do, of how you will achieve your goal. Now, what often comes to mind when you start thinking of what you should be doing? You may start finding certain doubts coming to mind—that you might not be able to do it or that you might fail. You then find that these doubts begin to trigger anxiety within you, and this anxiety will take the form of depression. You know that you cannot be very effective when you are depressed; and, in fact, you usually begin to have negative results at this point. The negative results will now come back to reinforce your doubts and convert them into negative convictions that you should not have tried in the first place. Further, your negative convictions will motivate you to avoid, retreat, or withdraw.

Now what did this entire process begin with? Thinking. Therefore your twenty-first technique is to stop thinking and use the technique called GOYA, or Getting Off Your Seat.

THINK

GOYA → How to do it → Doubts → You might fail →

Anxiety → Depression → Ineffectiveness →

Negative Results → Negative Convictions →

Motivates → Quitting

Whenever you find that thinking of what you should be doing causes this kind of negative chain reaction, then stop thinking and just act. Do it, and before you know it you will have started. Once you have done it, then your negative self-image can no longer say you cannot do it and your positive self-image can concern itself with how you can do it better. The GOYA technique applies to jumping off a diving board, telephoning someone when you feel unsure of yourself, running a mile, or giving a speech. Whenever thinking causes anxiety—which motivates you to avoid—just GOYA and do it!

22. Outer Symbols

If you are still failing, it is because you are so dependent on others that you cannot try to achieve on your own. But this primary obstacle can actually work to your advantage through the twenty-second technique, which is outer symbols. This technique requires that you find something external to yourself to depend on. I personally do not believe in using this technique because one should find his strength within himself rather than depend on people or objects around him. Nevertheless, *this technique does work*.

The kind of car you drive and where you live has a significant influence on how you feel about yourself. Doesn't wearing new clothes make you feel better, more confident and expansive? Doesn't a new car make you feel more sure of yourself and more ambitious about reaching new levels of success? While you may find the thought objectionable, it is a fact that when a person buys a more expensive car he often begins to see himself as more successful and will therefore tend to *do better*. It is also true that when a person buys a more expensive house than he can afford, the house reminds him of his new status and he finds himself working harder to afford the home. Equally, a home can be an excellent investment and hedge against inflation because it usually increases in value, the taxes and interest are tax deductible, and the principal creates forced savings.

The right kind of clothing will not only make you feel more expansive about yourself and what you are doing but can also create a greater impact on people, which can result in increased sales. Everybody likes to be involved with successful people. At the same time, of course, it is important that we do not project ourselves in such a way that it threatens people, whether in the car we drive or in the clothing that we wear. For this reason we should not wear flashy clothing when selling in a conservative market as our customers may feel that we do not relate to them.

Many people are so unsure of themselves that they go too far in using this technique, depending on all sorts of lucky charms or status symbols for a sense of strength and success. Yet there are many outer symbols that, while external, are worth depending on if they get you started. It is good to identify with people who represent the kind of personality you would like to have. It is also worthwhile to identify with ideas that have made others succcessful. Alsu, when you are buying something, you might as well buy something that represents the kind of image that you would like to have of yourself.

23. Reward

The twenty-third technique is reward. Decide what gift you will give yourself if you achieve your goal. Get a picture of the present you intend to give yourself and put it in a place where it will serve as a continual reminder of where you want to be in the future and why you need to make sacrifices in the present. Your gift to yourself might be intangible, but whatever it is, decide at this time how you will reward yourself if you achieve your goal.

24. Punishment

Your last technique is punishment. Decide at this time what you will take away from yourself, discontinue, or sacrifice if you do not achieve your goal. Then, when you think of avoiding your objective, the punishment that you have planned for yourself may cause enough stress to force you to continue. This can be combined with commitment to others by telling another what you plan to give up.

Repetition

From this day forward, whenever you wish to achieve a goal, apply these twenty-four techniques. Begin with positive affirmations and, as you feel that you need more assistance, continue through the list until you find the right combination of techniques to achieve your goal. I would also like you to keep in mind the fact that you have spent many years becoming the kind of person that you are today. The techniques presented here are correct, and yet you have to realize that you still may not succeed the first time you try them. You may succeed immediately, but you have to realize that it might take a few days or a few weeks before you are able to change your image, attitudes, or habits.

An example of the importance of repetition is found in the story of a woman who wanted to make some money on the side, so she opened up a "sporting house." She decided to specialize, so she rented a building with three floors. On the first floor she had nurses catering to medical personnel. On the second floor she had telephone operators whose specialty was businessmen. On the third floor she had schoolteachers to accommodate intellectuals. After a few months she was doing very well—except that all the money was coming from the third floor. She wanted to discover what the problem was, so she concealed microphones on the first floor one night and overheard the nurses continuously saying, "Hold still, sir, this won't hurt a bit." She could see where this could cause a problem, so on the second night she put the microphones in with the telephone operators, and one thing she constantly overheard was, "You have three minutes left, sir." She could see where this caused difficulty, so on the third night she put microphones in with the schoolteachers so she could find out what they were doing correctly and she constantly overheard them saying, "If you don't get it right this time, we're going to do it over and over again until you get it right."

That is what I am talking about. If you do not succeed at first, then I want you to do it over and over again until you get it right. You have spent many years becoming the kind of person you are today. If you want to change, you will often have to be willing to try more than once in order to succeed.

X

A Workshop Section

There are five goals that you should achieve if you wish to fulfill your potential and satisfy all your needs. They are as follows:

1. I never see failure as failure but only as that which I must go through to succeed.
2. When I feel threatened by someone, I always react—but in a disarming way.
3. I enjoy converting anxiety into creative energy.
4. I enjoy changing.
5. I am continually achieving new levels of success.

The goal achieving techniques that you have just studied should assure you of achieving these goals as well as any other goal you aim for in life. The following workshop section should increase your effectiveness in using these powerful goal-achieving techniques. The first is to solve the problem of being oversensitive to failure or rejection.

1. Positive Affirmation
   I never see failure as failure but only as that which I have to go through to succeed.
2. Descriptive Technique
   Describe in detail how you react positively to failure experi-

111

ences. For example, "Whenever I fail, I first ask myself why I lasted as long as I did. Then I ask myself what I could have done to last longer. Whenever I have not achieved my objectives in a specific day I ask myself, 'Am I afraid of failure?' and then I try again, if for no other reason than to prove to myself that failure cannot stop me. I constantly remind myself of the positive attitudes toward failure."

3. Incentive Technique
   List the benefits to be derived by overcoming your fear of failure:
   a. I am more consistently successful.
   b. I impress people with my ability to persevere and succeed.
   c. Failure will no longer cause anxiety.
   d. I am able to respect myself.

4. Fear Technique
   List the disadvantages that you'll have to face if you do not change your attitude toward failure:
   a. I will continue to experience anxiety when I fail or am rejected.
   b. I will create a negative impact on people because of my lack of ability to persevere.
   c. I will too often experience peaks and valleys rather than consistent success.
   d. I will all too often disrespect myself for my inability to handle failure and rejection.

5. Total Commitment
   I am totally committed to approaching failure as no more than that which I have to go through to succeed.

6. Vivid Imagination
   From this day forward, whenever I attempt to achieve in a situation in which I have traditionally been afraid of failure, I shall initially imagine myself succeeding. I shall also imagine myself persevering when I do fail because I visualize myself deserving success.

7. Defense Mechanism
   Determine what defense mechanism you are using that, while protecting you from failure, is also blocking you from achieving your objectives. Do you become very empathetic or aggressive? How do you protect yourself from failure, and how could you develop the kind of protective devices that would also assure your success?

8. The Obstacle
   Realizing that your fear of failure is based on your need for

acceptance should help you to better understand the tremendous importance of accepting yourself. In this way you will no longer be so concerned about the reaction of others as to become ineffective when you do not get positive feedback.

9. Strength Bombardment
   Make a list of your strengths as well as your past successes in an effort to impress upon yourself the reason why you should succeed, regardless of what temporary setbacks you may experience.

10. Positive Thinking
    Make a list of all the advantages you may gain when you fail, such as:
    a. I gain the negative feedback that I need in order to make a change in my course.
    b. It brings me more quickly to the prospect who will buy.
    c. I create more activity, which assures me of greater income.
    d. I gain the opportunity to experiment with new techniques and improve my repertoire of approaches.

11. Challenge Thinking
    You must realize that if you were never confronted with failure experiences, you would never have the opportunity to test yourself and develop new strengths.
    The greater the chance of failure, the greater the opportunity of proving how capable you can be.

12. Obstacle Conversion
    How could you take the fear "I am afraid of rejection," and convert it into a strength? One way: "I am inspired by the challenge of gaining acceptance" or "I reject rejection." Develop your own positive thought.

13. Acceptance Span
    If you cannot overcome your fear of failure, then at least decide how much failure you could handle in order to begin to overcome fear. Could you make at least ten calls a day? How about five? What could you *believe* in order to begin to change?

14. Tailored Technique
    What techniques could you develop that would help you to disengage the fear of failure? Maybe if *you rejected yourself first* by saying, "I hope I am not calling at the wrong time, but I would like to present a few ideas to you that might be of some benefit. Do you have the time now?" It is difficult to reject a salesman who has already rejected himself, which is what you have done in this situation. This technique gets you through the fear, and if you do not care for this particular ap-

proach, then brainstorm with your associates or develop a technique on your own that is compatible with your personality.

15. Self-competition
One of your major goals has to be positive momentum, which is created when—each day—you do more than in the previous day. How much failure can you tolerate before you want to quit? If you can handle a little more today than yesterday, you will create the kind of momentum that will bring you to success. Determine the importance of each of your activities through a point system. How many points will you devote to dialing the phone, sending out a direct mail piece, gaining an appointment, making a presentation, closing, and every other important activity? Then try to score more points today than you did yesterday, and through this kind of self-competition you *have* to assure yourself of continuous success.

16. Leadership
Find someone in your office who is having difficulty handling failure and rejection and try to help him overcome his problem by using the same techniques discussed in this section, particularly by working on projects that tend to be threatening. This may force you into the success patterns that you need.

17. Commitment to Others
If you tell of the goals you want to achieve, you may find yourself with no choice but to pursue them. You might be afraid of rejection from prospects, but if you make a commitment to your spouse or boss, then your fear of being rejected by them if you do *not* achieve your goal may force you to succeed.

18. Competition
Think of someone you know who has the same fear of failure that you do and challenge him to compete with you in overcoming the problem. As an example, see who can gain the most number of prospecting calls. Again, you may want to decide on a point system for activity—such as each prospect that you contact being worth 1 point and every appointment being worth 5 points—and see how many points each of you can score each day. Through competition, you will realize that you are not the only one who has a fear of failure, and in the competition you may no longer dwell as much on your own frustrations.

19. "Acting as If"
Self-confidence overwhelms the fear of failure. You can achieve this ingredient for success if you can get people to treat you as though you *were* confident—but how can you do this if you

don't feel confident? By "acting as if." Just fake it. Make believe you are confident by projecting confidence and you will find that people will begin to treat you as an authority. This will help you to establish success patterns and win you true confidence within yourself, eliminating the fear of failure.

20. Exaggeration

Have you heard of snake therapy? People with an unreasoning fear of snakes are put in a small room by themselves, a room filled with snakes that are, of course, harmless. Since nothing happens to the individual that could hurt him, he gradually has to come to realize that his fears are injustified. While this may seem to you to be a radical approach, I will recommend it when it comes to your fear of overcoming failure. If you immersed yourself in cold calls for a single day, you might find that twenty cold calls from that day on are no longer so difficult. When I first started selling in the garment section of New York I once made 105 cold calls. From that day on 10 or 15 cold calls would never bother me.

21. GOYA

If all else fails, then you must admit that the reason you are having difficulty is that every time you think of what you should be doing you are triggering your doubts. This generates anxiety, which causes ineffectiveness and leads to negative results —justifying your doubts and converting them into negative convictions that motivate you to avoid your tasks and quit. If you come down to the twenty-first technique and all else has failed, then it is this negative cycle that is probably causing your difficulty. For this reason you must stop thinking about it and use my GOYA (getting off your seat) technique. Just do it. Before you know it you have made the effort and can no longer say "I can't do it" but rather, "How can I do even better?"

22. Outer Symbols

What could you depend on outside of yourself that would help you gain the inner confidence you need in order to overcome the fear of failure? Maybe a certain type of clothing would give you greater confidence in yourself. Maybe prospecting with a fellow salesman who has no difficulty handling failure might be just the boost you need to get you started. A crutch, maybe, but only a temporary one. You can also merge this technique with the "acting as if" technique. Find someone who has the characteristics you'd like to have and study how he acts. Then practice projecting the way he does.

23. Reward

What gift would you give yourself if you overcame your fear of failure? Having a reward if you achieve this goal may be just the incentive you need to keep you striving when you feel discouraged.

24. Punishment

Equally, you should decide what sacrifices you are going to make as long as you are not overcoming your fear of failure, as well as the punishment you will impose on yourself if you do not achieve the goal at all. Maybe this kind of irritation will cause enough stress to force you into it.

XI

Alpha-level Conditioning

More and more attention is being devoted to the brain, particularly as it relates to learning and the dynamics of change. In a study of the human mind, it has been determined that there are many different levels of the brain. Even sleep has more than one level. Recent research into sleep indicates that the mind is constantly active, and while you may think that you do not dream frequently, it is now known that you dream off and on throughout the night. You go through different levels of dreams, depending on the level of the mind. Just as there are different levels of sleep, there are also different levels of consciousness. You know that if you are driving along the road at night, you may become very sleepy, and all of a sudden you have no recollection of the last 5 miles, just as though you had been asleep! If a car had driven in front of you and forced you to react, there would be no doubt in your mind that you *had* been awake. During the day you find yourself in very active periods mentally, and then at times you may have periods of daydreaming, in which you are not very sharply awake.

Different Brain Levels

Recently electroencephalogram machines have detected different types of electrical activity in the brain at various levels of consciousness. When awake, the individual is at a beta level, which varies at

117

different frequencies. When asleep, the individual is at a theta level, in which there also are different levels of frequency. It has also been discovered that as the individual is either falling asleep or waking up, he is at an alpha level. At this particular level he has experiences that are similar to those of a person who is experiencing transcendental meditation, yoga, autosuggestion, hypnosis, or who is under the influence of certain drugs or alcohol. The significance of this alpha level is that the individual is not conscious enough to question suggestions that are made to him by others or himself and yet conscious enough to be aware of the suggestions and react to them.

People who believe in transcendental meditation deny that it is the same as hypnosis, just as people who believe in hypnosis may deny that it is the same as alpha conditioning. In the same way, people who believe in alpha conditioning do not agree that it is the same as transcendental meditation. But the techniques are basically the same. They all aim to get the individual beyond his conscious mind in terms of his self-image—both negative and positive—beyond his inhibitions, fears, or doubts. It is at the conscious level of the mind that the individual's thoughts will provoke energy and anxiety, and it is these emotions that stimulate the physical system. As the individual drops below this conscious level, he stops thinking; thus energy and anxiety are no longer triggered and the physical system begins to "fall asleep." At the same time the technique which is used allows the individual enough consciousness to achieve the objectives that he had in mind, and these objectives can be almost infinite in variety. They will be discussed later in this chapter.

Before examining how these techniques can benefit you—and before exploring the techniques that can help you achieve your objectives—I think you should first realize why your attitude toward such techniques may not be entirely positive. The term *alpha conditioning* is relatively new, and therefore it probably does not have any negative connotations for you. Transcendental meditation may cause you to react negatively if you are turned off by metaphysics or Eastern religion. Hypnosis would probably carry greater negative connotations, and for a number of reasons.

Fears of Hypnosis

One of the most common fears is that the person hypnotized will be made to appear foolish. The only experience most people have had with hypnosis is in stage shows where someone runs through the audience searching for his belly button. This type of theatrical performance results in negative associations that dissuade many people from capitalizing on hypnosis.

If the idea of hypnosis leads you to have this kind of negative reaction, then think of its successful use in the medical field. It is being used by dentists in order to eliminate pain and for the same purpose in childbirth. You may visit a dentist once a year, and a woman may give birth a few times in her life, but *you* may experience psychological pressures and mental blocks frequently, and these reduce your effectiveness.

Another fear that a person may have about hypnosis is that someone else will be in control of his mind, which is what happens when an individual becomes so suggestible as to readily accept most or all of the hypnotist's suggestions. In self-hypnosis, your purpose is to control yourself by becoming suggestible to your own thoughts. You know that very often it is your own fears and anxieties that control and motivate you, not your own inner desire to achieve and fulfill your potential. For this reason, if you really want to control yourself, you have to be able to get beyond your fears and anxiety. Techniques of suggestion will help you do just that.

Some people are worried about using hypnosis because they fear they will lose awareness of themselves. Actually, we find that most people at a conscious level have little awareness of themselves in the sense of really understanding what motivates and demotivates them. By reaching the alpha level, you can become more aware of yourself. One of the major reasons for this lack of conscious self-awareness is that the individual is distracted by fears or doubts that he has about himself. They distract him to such an extent that he has difficulty thinking or making a creative decision. These fears and doubts will also bottle up the strengths and abilities he has within him. By reaching the alpha level, you will be able to relax and get beyond these distractions. In fact, that is hypnosis: the ability to relax your mind and body to such an extent that you go beyond your conscious blocks and reach a high degree of suggestibility. In self-hypnosis, one becomes highly suggestible to one's own thoughts.

Another objection people have to hypnosis is that it can be dangerous when practiced by an unqualified individual or by oneself. Obviously, if you are successful in reaching this level of self-suggestion, you must see to it that the suggestions are constructive, regardless of whether you are hypnotizing yourself or being hypnotized by someone else. As an example, if you are smoking to eliminate anxiety and you use alpha-level conditioning to stop smoking, what will happen to the anxiety? You may find yourself becoming very irritable and eating heavily in an effort to eliminate the irritation. Now you must put yourself under hypnosis again in order to stop eating excessively—and thus you may start drinking in order to eliminate the resulting anxiety. You then put yourself under hypnosis in order to stop drinking and now find yourself taking up sex! So the problem may get worse or better—depending on your viewpoint—if you do not understand all the dynamics that are involved.

We live in an age of suggestibility, an age in which advertising and new forms of communication can influence our thinking about how we should live, think, and behave. You must accept the fact that suggestion does influence your life and you should learn how to control it, rather than allowing it to control you without your knowledge. In hypnosis or self-hypnosis you are dealing with the same process, but one that allows *you* to control the results.

Further, some people are fearful of their own inner thoughts. If they relax, they may reach into repressed thoughts that are disturbing. Yet getting to know yourself can also help you to understand the causes of your problems and to find their solutions. It is particularly unfortunate that so many people go through life without finding out—for fear they may discover something unpleasant—who they are. By accepting the challenge to know yourself better, you can develop your potential.

Some people fear that they may not awaken from the hypnotic state. In the deeper stages of the alpha level you are aware of yourself and have control. You may be tempted not to awaken only because you find it so pleasant where you are. Again, the alpha level is not a true sleep but more of a twilight zone between the conscious and subconscious levels; therefore emerging from the alpha level is not exactly the same as awakening, since you were not exactly asleep. Nevertheless, the similarities between alpha level and sleep are close enough that the term *awaken* is reasonably appropriate.

In learning to reach this alpha level, you may actually fall asleep and then wake up as you normally do. It is possible to slip from a hypnotic state into actual sleep because you are already conditioned to fall asleep when you become very relaxed. For this reason you should not use the technique late at night unless it is to program a particular thought into your subconscious as you are going to sleep. If you are taking a nap, you can use the technique to get a better rest in a shorter time and awaken when you want to. If there is any problem, you will just go through a normal sleep process.

The common situation which we have just discussed is that in which the individual finds the session so pleasant that he does not want to awaken. Nevertheless, people have the ability to wake themselves at a specific time, whether at 6:30 in the morning or in fifteen minutes.

Hypnosis, Alpha Level, and Suggestion

In the July 1970 issue of *Psychology Today,* an article discussed the claim that hypnosis does not exist but that suggestion does. Therefore any technique of hypnosis, alphaconditioning, or transcendental meditation might be synonymous with suggestion. But your objectives while in this state of hypnosis, meditation, or alpha-level conditioning may vary. The techniques of suggestion and its applications are two different subjects.

Benefits of Alpha Level

Before discussing techniques that can help you to reach the alpha level rapidly, I would like to discuss the benefits you can gain by reaching this level of your inner mind. The techniques of suggestion will be more meaningful to you if you first become interested in the benefits that you can gain from them.

There are two major benefits to be gained. The first is to increase your awareness of yourself in a number of particularly important areas, and the second is to increase your ability to change through the use of mind-conditioning techniques while at an alpha level. There are a number of questions that you should answer if you are going to become more aware of yourself, and they can be answered without being at an alpha level. Nevertheless, it is interesting to watch an individual's response change as he moves from a sharply awakened state of consciousness to an alpha level of consciousness or even to subconscious dreaming. For specific reasons, it is often difficult to answer most of these questions honestly; and when you attempt to be honest your answers will often be defensive or superficial. As you use techniques that create an alpha level of consciousness, you get below your fears or inhibitions and thus are able to answer the questions directly.

Levels of Self-awareness

You have had the experience of being asked a question in a challenging way, and invariably you gave an answer which was more defensive than truthful. If someone spends some time in developing rapport with you and you feel at ease with this individual, you may find yourself answering questions more freely—the same kinds of questions that you previously answered defensively. In fact, if you become very relaxed with someone, you may say things about yourself that you later wish you had not mentioned!

You can have the same type of experience at a party, where on arriving you find yourself in a strange group and are particularly careful about what you say. When asked questions about your work, you may often exaggerate in an effort to impress; and—rather than being yourself—you will be doing considerable role playing. As you have a couple of drinks, you will begin to relax and do less role playing. Now your comments may tend to be more reflective of your own inner desires than of an effort to be accepted. If you have enough drinks, you may find yourself expressing your innermost fears and desires to strangers.

Alcohol is one of many things that can create suggestibility because it very specifically slows down your thought process and thus reduces the anxiety that inhibitions create in you. Fears trigger the inhibitors within your nervous system, and these in turn trigger anxiety that keeps you alert and defensive. As alcohol or anything else that relaxes the thought process begins to take effect, the inhibiting thoughts are reduced. Therefore less inhibitors are operating and there is less anxiety. When the anxiety is reduced, your mind begins to drift downward from a conscious level to a subconscious level. This also happens when you fall asleep.

It is interesting to watch the personality changes of the individual as he becomes influenced by alcohol, as his behavior changes reflect the different levels of the mind. At a purely inhibited level, he will tend to role play for defensive purposes. As he begins to relax, he will reach his "irritation level," in which he will express his frustrations about anything which might be bothering him or, in a positive sense, anything which might be exciting him at the moment. Because he is reaching the first level of relaxation, he will express himself without particularly caring whether he appears irritable or whether he is playing the right role. Often an individual will have difficulty reaching a significant alpha level, or for that matter falling asleep, because as he begins to relax he quickly reaches this irritation level. If there are serious irritants at this level, they may cause enough anxiety to make it very difficult for him to become any more relaxed. Nevertheless, it can be very worthwhile to be able to get beyond your role-playing or first level and down to your irritation or second level so that you can better determine what is irritating you and distracting you from total effectiveness.

I have had the experience of trying to work on a project while feeling irritated. Whatever irritates me distracts me from my objective. By reaching the alpha level, I can quickly determine what the irritant might be so that I can decide the best way to eliminate its cause. In this way I can effectively channel my energies in order to achieve my objective.

At the third level the individual will express his opinions about the world and himself, which are a reflection of his self-image. For this reason, when you reach this level of your mind, you can gain a great deal of insight into your feelings about your own personal worth within any area of your life.

At the fourth level of the mind you reach the area of repressed thoughts. This might consist of negative thoughts that your positive self-image will not allow you to consider consciously and equally it may consist of positive thoughts that your negative self-image is repressing.

Within another area of the mind and not necessarily on a deeper level than the ones discussed previously is the memory of past experiences. If the individual is at his role-playing level, he will tend to recall those thoughts that justify his role playing. If he is at the second level, he will recall those experiences which justify his irritations or those that might be "turning him on." Experiences that are of considerable importance because they justify the positive or negative self-image will be expressed within the third level. And if they tend to be experiences that are the cause of his repressed thoughts, they will be expressed when he reaches to the fourth and deeper levels of his mind. The most provocative thoughts are the repressed thoughts that come from the fourth level of the mind. When these thoughts are expressed, they will often sound like those of a completely different individual because they are competing with the image he has of himself—his primary personality. Thus when he hears himself revealing repressed thoughts, he often finds it hard to believe it is himself speaking!

Understanding Yourself

One of the major applications of alpha-level conditioning is in understanding yourself. If you can answer the questions in this chapter, you will be in a better position to change. Your first question: Where do you see yourself in the future?

_____

_____

_____

In a hypnotic state the individual is often disturbed to find that *his dreams for the future are often very different from what he consciously believes he is after.* If you ask yourself where you want to be in the future, you will usually describe the kind of life-style that you consciously want because of past conditioning by society. You consciously want to live in a particular neighborhood with a particular kind of job, a certain kind of car, a particular vacation, and certain kinds of recreational and social activities. In a hypnotic state the individual often dreams of a house on a hill all by itself, with no one around and the wind blowing through meadowland.

Everything is quiet and still and there are no goals, no effort, no anxiety. It seems to symbolize the inner need to be comfortable and to have peace of mind. This, of course, conflicts with the conscious need to strive toward socially acceptable goals. It is possible that if you are experiencing this kind of conflict, it may be the primary reason for the dilution of your energies and the fact that you are not the laser beam of energy that you could be. Therefore you need to strive toward balance while at the same time allowing yourself enough "comfort" to enjoy the process of achieving. Further, your ability to attain your consciously conditioned goals can increase your ability to reach goals of comfort.

Do not allow these thoughts to influence you as you ask yourself the same question while trying one of the suggested alpha-level techniques in the next chapter, for people often have entirely different dreams. Frequently the dreams revolve around the inner desire to be successful in a very particular area of life which symbolizes a specific value system. As an example, if the individual has a tremendous need for recognition and his value system tends to relate to politics, he will see himself succeeding in politics and gaining the recognition that he needs. Answer this first question and the following questions briefly and leave room for an additional response after you have again answered these questions at the alpha level.

Self-awareness: Defense Mechanisms

Question two: Imagine that you are walking down a country road and have lost your way. You see a cottage up ahead and you stop and knock at the door. The individual inside is wary of you and therefore afraid to answer the door. This upsets you because you only want directions. What would you do in a situation like this?

_____

_____

_____

Question three: Imagine now that you are walking down that same road again and you see someone ahead of you. As he approaches you, he stops you and asks for your money. What would you do in a situation like this?

_____

_____

_____

Answer these last two questions before reading any further. Now, did you find an interesting similarity in the two questions? If you are very anxious for the person to answer the door and you do not particularly mind the individual who approaches you on the road, it may indicate a fear of being alone to the point where you do not even care what kind of contact you may have with people as long as you are not alone. If you do not particularly care whether the person answers the door and you continue on your own, disregarding the person in the road as though he really were not there, it may indicate that you tend to be a very self-sufficient individual to the point where you often have difficulty creating a healthy give-and-take relationship with people. If you were very aggressive at the door and yet yielded to the stranger that you met, it may indicate that you attack only when there is no resistance and give in if you confront resistance. If you do not particularly react at the door but overreact with the stranger, it may indicate that you become more active when challenged and that, when unchallenged, you tend not to react. These are but a few of the possible insights that can be gained by answering these two questions.

Self-awareness: Self-appreciation

Question four: I would like you to imagine that you have just been introduced to someone who looks just like you and who, as you speak with him, turns out to sound just like you. How do you feel about this individual?

_____

_____

_____

In a hypnotic state this is very often a difficult question to answer. People at the alpha level frequently are unable to imagine themselves, giving the impression that they are subconsciously avoiding the question. The individual may wake up or fall asleep rather than remain at this alpha level, or everything may become hazy to him. Anything to avoid asking himself how he feels about himself. If you found it difficult to answer this question, it is understandable, for we often are reluctant to confront ourselves. As you succeed in getting beyond your own inhibitions you may, through your ability to use your imagination spontaneously, gain a new insight into your own behavior once you determine how you feel about yourself.

Self-awareness: Obstacle

Question five: What is holding you back from being as effective as you could be?

_____

_____

_____

If you try to answer this question at a very conscious level you will probably fall back on defense mechanisms rather than actual obstacles. You will mention such "acceptable" things as being lazy, procrastinating, or not yet being as competent in your field as you need to be. As you begin to relax and reach your irritation level, you may feel that your major obstacle is the fact that people do not understand you or that someone in your past blocked you from an opportunity that may have been available at a particular time. Further relaxed, you begin to reach your self-image level, where you may now realize that the reason you are not as successful as you should be is that you have some doubts about yourself within a particular area of responsibility—thus, a negative self-image. More relaxed still and moving to the fourth level, you may become aware of repressed fears, such as a fear of rejection, which might be the reason for part of your image becoming negative.

Self-awareness: Negative Experiences

Question six: What experiences have you had in your past that might have created your present obstacle?

_____

_____

_____

Perhaps no *one* experience is responsible for your present obstacle, but there might be one that symbolizes the cause of the problem. Invariably it is one in which you failed or met rejection, and it had a negative effect on your image of yourself. This caused you to avoid similar situations ever after and therefore limits your effectiveness. Again, *the main point is not the experience but the way you react to the experience that determines whether you develop weaknesses or strengths.* Sometimes the best experience an individual has is a negative one because he reacts to it positively, thus developing the ability to react positively to future problems.

Often we find that there is no major negative experience, and that is the cause of present difficulties. The individual was never prepared to handle problems. The specific experiences that cause a problem are myriad. Some experiences make us want to be liked by people or to avoid being rejected, and thus we spend more time in trying to please people than in fulfilling our own potential. In other cases, we may have succeeded in childhood by fighting back and now spend too much of our time attacking people. Some experiences motivate us to want to impress people, and thus we spend too much of our time trying to impress others and too little achieving the kinds of goals that can really fulfill our potential. We may have had success with empathy, and now we may spend too much time being empathetic in order to protect ourselves and too little acting decisively in order to succeed.

Self-awareness: Repressed Thoughts

Question seven: What major thoughts are you subconsciously repressing?

_____

_____

_____

Of course, it would not be logical for you to be able to answer this question on a conscious level. It would require successful alpha-level conditioning to supply the required insight, and even then you might have difficulty recalling your answer as you awake. At the alpha level the individual often has the experience of recalling something, and then, as he awakes, it is almost as though he heard a voice within him saying, "I'm sorry but you cannot leave with this information." You've probably had a similar experience waking up in the morning and clutching at the tag end of a dream you wanted to recall, only to have the dream seem to slip from your consciousness. This particular problem will occur more frequently when you are trying to bring repressed thoughts to your conscious mind.

Self-awareness: Untapped Potential

Question eight: What strengths could you use more effectively?

_____

_____

_____

This should be a rather easy question to answer at a conscious level, and as you relax you will find that the answer may change and become even more significant. For the empathetic individual it might mean using the decisiveness that he has but is reluctant to use.

Self-awareness: Positive Experiences

Question nine: What experiences have you had in your past that are responsible for your present success?

_____

_____

_____

It is worthwhile to know why you are successful so that you may better capitalize on your strengths. Equally, the positive experiences you've had in the past may cause certain of your abilities to become so strong that you lose balance. If you are successful today because in childhood you were very decisive in a threatening situation, you now may be too decisive and tend to threaten people. If you understand what positive experiences you have had, then you might understand why you are strong in some areas and lacking in others.

Self-awareness: Solutions

Question ten: What experiences do you need to have today that will make you more effective?

_____

_____

_____

In a conscious state you may not want to recognize what you need to do to become more effective because the idea of what you should be doing may threaten you. As you become more relaxed and feel less threatened, you will probably realize what action you should be taking at this time in order to become more successful.

Techniques for Reconditioning

Having answered these ten self-awareness questions, you are prepared for the second and last stage of this subject, and that is how to change. At an alpha level you are highly responsive to two specific techniques that can help you to change your image of yourself. The first technique is *positive affirmation*.

In the stage show the hypnotist will say, "You are as straight as a board, as rigid as a piece of steel," and the subject stretches out between two chairs. In dentistry or childbirth the patient is told, "You feel no pain." If the individual has been brought to a level of high suggestibility, *that particular thought is accepted by his subconscious mind and he behaves accordingly.* If *you* can reach a level of high suggestibility and give a suggestion to yourself in the form of a positive affirmation, your subconscious will have to assume that it is true and you will find your behavior changing. If what you wish to accomplish is within your potential, the positive affirmation will work!

There could be one stumbling block—and that is in your own negative self-image. In a sense, there is a conflict between the desire of your positive self to change and that of your negative self to resist change. Your ability to succeed with this technique is first dependent on the strength of your negative self-image. If you wish to lose 10 pounds and you have succeeded before, obviously your image is not all that negative; so it would require very little suggestibility on your part to get beyond whatever negative image might exist. On the other hand, if you wish to stop smoking but have been smoking heavily for thirty years and have failed many times to stop smoking, your image of yourself is probably very negative within this area. For this reason you will have to become very receptive to your own suggestions and reach a significantly deep level of your mind before you can get beyond this negative self-image and begin to succeed with the positive affirmation, "I am a nonsmoker."

If you feel disbelief as you make the suggestion or find that you are not acting upon it, try applying the acceptance-span technique and decide how much you could believe. If you cannot believe in losing 10 pounds, would you believe 5 pounds? Make that suggestion to yourself. Regardless of what you wish to achieve in life, there will always be some part of your goal that is believable. By beginning at that point you can create a momentum that will help you to achieve at least a significant part of your goal.

The second major mind-conditioning technique that can be used to change your self-image is vivid imagination. As discussed before, your subconscious mind cannot tell the difference between a real and an imagined thought. At the alpha level it is particularly easy to imagine yourself succeeding in specific situations, and your subconscious will assume that what you imagined is true and will act accordingly. Again, this depends on how negative your self-image within the area you wish to change may be. If your image is particularly negative, you may have to strain to imagine yourself succeeding or to believe what you imagined; and in this case your sub-conscious will not react positively. Again, you should imagine only what you can believe in order to begin to change.

Applications

The applications for these techniques are as numerous as the unused abilities within your potential. Edison could sleep only two hours at night and, by taking a twenty-minute deep sleep every three or four hours as he found himself becoming tired and losing his creativity, was able to work almost twenty hours. I am sure you've all too often had the experience of coming home in the evening so tired as not to be able to enjoy your evening or do anything in particular except watch television and eat. In addition, when you did try to sleep you were so tired you couldn't sleep or slept poorly and woke up tired the next morning. You can learn to relax rapidly and fall into a deep sleep within a matter of seconds, just as Edison did. You can suggest to yourself that you will wake up in twenty minutes, and when you wake you will be very refreshed for at least three or four hours. In this way you can restore your energy and work at a highly creative level for many hours; and when you go to sleep you will fall asleep easily, have a better sleep, and need less sleep.

If you find yourself irritated during the day, you can use the technique for a few minutes to calm yourself down. As you fall asleep at night, you can program within your mind how you will feel the next morning, what time you will wake up, positive affirmations that you wish to achieve, or specific questions that you would like to answer through dreams which you will recall when you awake the next morning. I am sure that you are already achieving many of these objectives, whether automatically or with some conscious effort. For this reason, you are already familiar with alpha conditioning and merely need to remind yourself of your ability to use it as well as of ideas that can help you use it more effectively.

XII

Alpha-level Techniques

There are many techniques that can be used for alpha conditioning, but before we discuss them you should, as a matter of preparation, be aware of certain thoughts. First of all, you should not *try*. You've had the experience of trying to go to sleep at night because you had to get up early the next morning, and the more you tried to fall asleep the more difficult it became. In preparing yourself for alpha conditioning techniques, you should not try or make any serious effort. You should take it in a relaxed and casual manner.

Actually, you are already proficient at reaching an alpha level. When you fall asleep at night, as well as when you awake, you go through an alpha level for at least a few seconds. You've had the experience of waking in the morning and for a moment not know what time of day it was, what day of the week, or even where you were. You should also realize the natural ability you have to completely shut down your conscious mind in a few moments and fall into a deep sleep that can last for hours. Now what do you do that allows you to fall asleep so quickly at night?

You stop trying and you banish all thoughts from your mind that might cause you to be "wound up." By eliminating thoughts you eliminate emotions, for emotions can be caused only by thoughts, and you quickly begin to relax. Thus your mind starts to fall asleep;

and by relaxing your muscles, your body begins to fall asleep. If you give attention to what is occurring, you will realize that you are beginning to dream—and you actually have no awareness of your body.

You must go through the alpha level before reaching a normal, deep sleep level. To reach the alpha level is easy—but to remain at the alpha level without falling asleep is not so simple. This is the challenge: How can you allow your body to fall asleep and your mind to dream spontaneously while still being consciously aware of what is occurring? You frequently have this experience while falling asleep or awakening, but the challenge is to hold at this alpha level. If you can do it, you can unlock "secrets" within your subconscious mind and significantly increase your ability to reprogram your self-image.

First Technique—Imagine a Candle

What causes hypnosis? A candle can create a hypnotic effect because it causes you to concentrate, but on what? On nothing but the candle, and that is important to realize if you are going to succeed in reaching the alpha level. The candle is effective because the more you concentrate on the candle the less you can think of anything else. If you stop thinking, the emotions that are triggered by thoughts will subside and your mind and body will begin to fall asleep. Yet you cannot really fall asleep because, as long as you are looking at the candle, your eyes are open and you must keep some level of consciousness, particularly since light is a stimulus that keeps you awake. Therefore anything that induces you to focus all your attention without thinking, and holds your attention while you relax, will directly cause you to reach and hold at an alpha level.

With these thoughts in mind, you are ready for your first alpha-level session. All I ask you to do as you read the next section is to be in a room by yourself where it is relatively quiet and to get yourself into a comfortable position. I do not want you to *try* or make any effort whatever.

Second—Imagine Driving

I am sure you have had the experience of driving along a country road late at night, and all of a sudden you realized that you had no recollection of the last 5 miles. You *were* awake, but not really. You were at a twilight-zone level of your mind where there were no thoughts, and you were operating unconsciously. What had happened?

Imagine yourself in such a situation now. You are alone and the road is straight, hardly a curve to distract you. Your lights search into the darkness and you concentrate on the monotony of the road. You have an excellent imagination. You can imagine the road with the lights alongside. The lights keep going by, keep going by, and you find yourself relaxing. The more you concentrate on the road the more you feel yourself drifting, just letting yourself go.

You become aware of the road as the cars on the other side go by. Monotonously they keep going by and you think of nothing but the endless road. Your mind relaxes and all your muscles become very comfortable. It seems as though your body were floating and your mind were beginning to drift.

As soon as you begin succeeding with this or any other technique, it indicates that you can allow your mind to drift without having to use any additional technique. Just close your eyes and continue to concentrate on that which appears to be relaxing you, and ask yourself a question and imagine the answer.

As you read all the techniques in this section, you should decide which you prefer, even if it is a combination of techniques that you develop on your own. Then you or someone else should tape-record the one you prefer. Listening to a tape recorder can allow you to close your eyes. That helps, but all too often it can be too helpful because it causes you to fall asleep, and that's not the objective. For this reason you must keep your mind on some point of interest that retains an element of thought. Many people find it difficult to reach this fascinating level of the mind. Yet the real problem is that the individual may go through the alpha level too quickly and fall asleep. Reaching the alpha level is easy; holding at that level is less so.

Third—Pleasant Setting

I would like you now to follow the next technique. Again, do not try, think, or make any effort. Just let yourself relax. The next technique is one of the best because it is based on your own past experiences and that which reminds you of a pleasant and comfortable feeling. There was a place in your childhood you were fond of because it was so quiet and relaxing. There was probably water, maybe a stream or a pond. Everything was green, maybe a meadowland with trees. You were alone and it was very peaceful; if you concentrate, you can probably recall the many soft sounds of birds and water and the muffled sounds that the wind made as it moved through the grass and trees. You have an excellent imagination, and you can recall how relaxing and pleasant it was to sit along the water and stare at a leaf that might be floating downstream. You can feel your muscles relaxing and a tingling sensation in your hands and feet. It is as though your body were falling asleep and your arms and legs were becoming so heavy that you could almost feel yourself sinking downward, downward, deeper and deeper, more and more relaxed. Just letting your mind drift without thinking or trying. Just letting yourself go.

There are a number of ways to test yourself as you begin to relax and reach the alpha level. The physical tests relate to those signs which indicate that your muscles are falling asleep. You're first aware of a relaxing effect. Then you may notice a loss of physical sensation—all you seem to be able to feel is the pressure of your body, but no tension. Mentally you have a sensation of drifting. Of particular importance is the experience of dreaming, in which you begin spontaneously to imagine things. In a broad respect the test is based on the sensation of sleeping: your body feels asleep and your mind dreams without effort, but you are still aware of what is happening.

Whether the device of imagining a pleasant scene from childhood was effective is secondary, as the next technique goes one step further. Here you create whatever you find relaxing. As I stimulate your thinking with a number of possibilities, you should take the one to which you relate most easily and at that point disregard me and go on on your own.

Fourth—Concentration on Nothing

As an example, have you ever stretched out on the rug after a pleasant dinner and stared at the fireplace? You are alone and comfortable, lying on your back, your head on pillows, everything dark and quiet except the flickering light and the crackling sound of that warm fire. Gradually there is the sensation of your muscles relaxing and your mind beginning to drift. If you can feel yourself beginning to relax, then follow your own imagination and disregard me.

If you still need help, imagine you are at the beach stretched out on the warm sand. You can feel the warm sun and a cool breeze that keeps you very comfortable. There is the roar of the surf, rolling in and rolling out. The surf is loud, and if you listen carefully you hear nothing else. The rhythmic sound distracts you from yourself until all you can feel is your mind wandering in and out like the surf. First you are awake, then sleeping, now less awake, now more relaxed. Do you feel your muscles relaxing and your mind beginning to drift? If so, follow your imagination and disregard me.

There are many variations of the "concentration on nothing" technique. Every technique presented in this section relates to this technique in some form. In transcendental meditation you are given a chant, and as you recite the chant you feel yourself concentrating only on it. The chant gradually replaces all thoughts which might trigger emotion, and thus you begin to relax. Yet you cannot fall asleep while chanting. With this kind of technique you can reach the alpha level and hold at that point. Those who approach meditation as a religion may take offense at this simplistic explanation. Nevertheless, the chant is a "concentration-on-nothing" technique that is excellent for alpha-level conditioning.

Counting sheep has the same effect. You are in bed in a relaxed position but you are having trouble falling asleep. Something positive or negative is on your mind and it is keeping you awake. You begin counting sheep, and gradually, without realizing it, you stop thinking of what has been keeping you awake. You are now thinking only of the sheep jumping over that fence, and counting, counting, counting until you slowly become relaxed. Your desire is to fall asleep, and since you are relaxed it is exactly what happens. For these reasons whenever you are practicing an alpha-level technique it is important to remind yourself that your desire is *not* to fall asleep, or you will.

One of the simplest and most effective techniques is staring at an unimportant object. Try it at this time. Stretch out and stare at the ceiling. Pick a spot that is small and meaningless and stare only at it. You will find that the more you concentrate on it the less you will think of anything else, thus relaxing quickly. As long as you keep staring at it you will lose all thoughts and emotions and therefore fall deeper and deeper into the alpha level of your mind. Yet as long as your eyes are open you cannot really fall asleep. You may have some rather unusual physical and mental experiences at this particular point.

Authority Technique

There are other techniques excluding drugs and alcohol. The most popular is the authority technique. The stage hypnotist says you are hypnotized. If you believe he can control you, your subconscious mind switches from your self-image to the hypnotist. The same occurs when the witch doctor tells the primitive Indian that he can walk barefoot over the hot coals and he does so without ill effects. This is because such a suggestion can significantly desensitize the skin to pain and heat.

If the witch doctor gave you the same suggestion, you would not believe him, as he is not your authority. Yet if you went to your doctor and he felt that your headache or stomachache was psychologically caused, he might give you a sugar pill which, because you believe in him, would relieve the pain immediately. Vice versa, if the primitive Indian went to your doctor, he probably would react just as negatively as you would to his witch doctor.

What you believe to be true will be assumed to be true by your subconscious mind. If it it within your ability, you will gain the results that have been suggested. It is simply mind over matter. The value of using concentration-on-nothing techniques is that they help *you* to become the authority rather than depending on someone else. In this way you can gradually condition yourself to reach an alpha level quickly and to determine what the suggestion should be. If you have difficulty with the suggestion, you can determine the cause and make alterations that resolve the problem.

Fifth—Muscle-relaxation Technique

Your next technique is a traditional one of hypnosis and a rather thorough approach. It is particularly appropriate for recording and playing back from tape. As you prepare yourself for this technique by getting yourself into a comfortable position, I would like to remind you that there should be no pressure on any part of your body. For this reason, if you are sitting, you should have your feet flat on the floor, your back rather erect, and your hands flat on your legs. In this way there is no significant pressure on any one part of your body to interfere with relaxation. As you do begin to relax, you can let your head fall forward and allow your shoulders and arms to sag. I would like you at this time to take a deep breath and hold it for a few seconds. You may feel the tension rising in your system, and as you now exhale slowly you will feel the tension leaving your system. Whether you want to or not, you will find yourself beginning to relax by taking a couple of deep breaths and exhaling slowly. This is because deep breathing, when not overdone, eliminates anxiety in the system and is therefore a physical technique of reaching the alpha level. Now that you are in a comfortable and relaxed position (it is preferable that you record onto a tape cassette and listen to the playback with your eyes closed), I would like you to imagine that you are standing at the top of ten thickly carpeted steps. I would like you to walk down these steps one stair at a time. On your first step I would like you to concentrate on the muscles in your feet. Your only thought is of the muscles in your feet; they are becoming very relaxed and comfortable. As they begin to relax, you can feel your feet sinking into that thick carpet.

Now, on your second step, become aware of all the muscles in your legs, your thigh muscles and your calf muscles. If you are going to think of anything at all I would like you to think of the muscles in your legs—they are becoming very relaxed. You feel as though there are weights on your legs and they are becoming very heavy, sinking deeper and deeper into that very thick carpet. Not a matter of trying or making any effort. Just let yourself go.

On your third step, if you are going to imagine anything at all,

I would like you to imagine all the muscles in your back becoming very relaxed. It feels as though they were sagging as you let go of yourself and all the tension leaves your body.

On your fourth step, if you are going to concentrate on anything at all, I would like you to concentrate on the muscles in your shoulders. They are becoming very relaxed as all the tension leaves the muscles in your shoulders. Very relaxed and very loose. As they relax you can feel yourself sinking deeper and deeper into that very thick carpet.

Now, on your fifth step, all the muscles in your neck are relaxing. As you relax, you feel yourself beginning to float. All the neck muscles are becoming heavy. There is a pleasant sensation of sinking deeper and deeper into this drifting state.

Now, on your sixth step, all the muscles in your face are relaxing. You can feel your cheek muscles relaxing as all the tension leaves the muscles in your face and scalp. If you are going to be aware of anything at all, I would like you to be aware of all the tension leaving the muscles in your face.

On your seventh step, all the muscles in your arms are relaxing. If you are going to think of anything at all, think of the muscles in your arms. They are becoming more and more relaxed. It is as though there were weights on your legs and they were becoming very heavy, sinking deeper and deeper into the very thick carpet as you just let yourself go.

On your eighth step, all the muscles in your hands are relaxing. If you are going to be aware of anything at all, I would like you to be aware of the muscles in your hands, how relaxed they are becoming. A pleasant sensation of floating and drifting downward.

On your ninth step, all the muscles in your body are relaxing. There is a tingling sensation in your hands and feet as all the tension leaves your body.

On your tenth step, you are more relaxed than you have ever been before. All the muscles in your body are relaxed, and you are sinking deeper and deeper into a very pleasant state of relaxation. Your mind is drifting and your body feels as though it were floating. You can feel a tingling sensation in your hands and feet. There is no thought or effort, just drifting.

Sixth—Visualization Technique

Your last technique I have found to be the most effective of all. Again I would like you to get into a comfortable position, allow your eyes to close as soon as you feel the tension leaving your eyes, and stop trying. If you find at any time with any of these techniques that there is tension in your eyes, then leave them open and just stare at a spot on the wall or ceiling in front of you until you feel yourself wanting to close your eyes. I would like you at this time to take one or two deep breaths, breathing in deeply, holding the breath for a moment, and then exhaling slowly.

You have an excellent imagination. You can imagine that you are walking down a hillside, through spring flowers and thick grass. You are walking down this trail, walking downward, downward, deeper and deeper, more and more relaxed. Down below you see a stream, the waters rushing over the rocks. I would like you to walk down toward the stream, and as you approach it I would like you to sit down alongside a tree and just watch the water, rushing downstream, downstream, downward, deeper and deeper, more and more relaxed.

As you sit there you will notice a leaf drifting down from the tree. The leaf is drifting down so slowly that it almost appears motionless, just as you can feel your mind beginning to drift downward, almost motionlessly, drifting downward, downward, more and more comfortable. Now the leaf reaches the surface of the stream and begins to move downstream, downstream, floating downstream on the surface of the water. Floating very gently downstream, just as you can feel yourself floating downward, downward, more and more comfortable, until the leaf reaches the surface of a pond. The water of the pond is very quiet and still. Surrounding the pond is a meadowland, the grass blowing slowly in a gentle wind. The wind slowly pushes the leaf across the quiet water of the pond. Toward the end of the pond is a whirlpool. The water of the whirlpool is turning slowly, very slowly. Now the leaf reaches the outer rim of that whirlpool and begins to slowly turn, turning downward, downward, deeper and deeper, and more and more relaxed. The leaf begins to spin more rapidly now, spinning downward, just as you can feel your own mind beginning to drift downward, letting go, feeling a very pleasant sensation of drifting downward. There is no feeling of danger. You can control the speed comfortably. It feels as though your mind were a cavern, and you are drifting back into the cavern of your own mind. You can feel yourself drifting backward now, backward, just letting yourself go. Drifting back into the cavern of your own mind. At this time I turn it over to you, to close your eyes and let your mind relax and achieve whatever objective you may have at this time.

With alpha-level conditioning you have a key to your subconscious potential that can unlock your abilities and strengths. For some it will be easy to master and they will reap immediate benefits; for others it will require patience. Remember, it is not a matter of trying or thinking but of just letting yourself go. It may be helpful if you can get a better idea of what this state of relaxation feels like. To capture some emotional sensation, you should recognize the stages you go through as you fall asleep. Notice how you turn out the lights, stretch out, close your eyes, let yourself go, stop thinking, and gradually slip off. As you fall asleep at night, try to recognize the alpha level. It may be difficult: every time you try to identify the stage you are at, you will have a tendency to wake up.

Do not be concerned about immediate and great success. What important skills have you learned in only a few minutes? You should also realize that it is not necessary to reach deep levels of suggestibility if the blocks you wish to eliminate—or the abilities you wish to use—are at easily accessible levels and require only a light state of suggestibility.

Another important consideration is that, once having succeeded in reprogramming yourself, you subsequently need only suggest to yourself what you wish to accomplish and you will immediately succeed without having to reach the alpha level. It is like a computer. When you are programming the computer it takes a great deal of time, but afterwards you just hit the button to get the results you are after. In this respect your mind is very similar. You will use hypnosis only when the conditioning or programming is not complete and needs varying degrees of reinforcement.

Remember that there is great potential within you and that through alpha-level conditioning you can begin to unlock this potential, allowing yourself to reach greater and often astonishing levels of achievement and personal satisfaction.

XIII

On Interpersonal Relations

Two Kinds of Relationships

What kind of relationship are you looking for with people? Are you interested in developing a pleasant one-to-one relationship, in which there is an equal give and take from you and the other individual; or are you interested in controlling the situation? These two factors have a dynamic impact on every major aspect of your life.

Take anxiety. If you are a one-to-one type of person seeking pleasant relationships with others and you experience anxiety, you will tend to become depressed. If you have to control the relationship in order to feel successful, then when you experience anxiety you will tend to become hostile. The one-to-one type of person becomes depressed because he does not want to express his emotions outwardly and risk losing the pleasant relationship he is seeking. The control type of person is not particularly concerned about *how* people feel about him as long as he can dominate the situation, and therefore is not in the least reluctant to become hostile. In fact, by converting his anxiety outwardly, he will tend to threaten people, which can help strengthen his position. Of course, the ideal situation is to convert the anxiety into creative energy.

Image Projection

The impression you create is determined primarily by the kind of relationships you seek. If you seek a pleasant one-to-one relationship, you will tend to project such characteristics as warmth, sensitivity, sympathy, receptiveness, sincerity, and emotional concern for others. If you tend to be a control type of individual, you will usually project such characteristics as aggressiveness, confidence, strength, and positiveness. But people want to know that you are sensitive to them. They also want to have confidence in you because you seem confident in yourself. The ideal situation is to project balance.

Defense Mechanisms

If someone threatens or challenges the one-to-one individual, he will tend to protect himself with such defense mechanisms as the "nice guy" game. He believes that if he plays the part of the nice guy, people will not feel threatened by him and therefore will have no reason to attack him. The control type of individual knows that his best defense is an attack. He believes that if he is going to control, then, if he is challenged by others, he must challenge them even more strongly. In this way he attempts to convince them that it is better to back off. Thus he controls. The ideal defense mechanism is to attack, but nicely.

Goals

When it comes to goals in life, the goal of the one-to-one individual is to be liked. The more people like him, the more he feels successful. The control type of individual has one primary goal in life, and that is power—which takes many forms. There is money power—such as income, investments, status symbols, and net worth. Then there is ego power, such as the size of his sales territory or his position of authority. Through money and ego power, the individual attains his goal of control. The ideal situation is to have one primary objective in life, and that is to fulfill your own potential. Otherwise you may be so concerned about pleasing people in order to be liked that you never fulfill your own potential; or you may be so interested in gaining power in order to influence others that you never achieve the kind of goals that could help you become self-sufficient.

Fears

The major fear of the one-to-one type is the fear of being rejected, for rejection is the opposite of being liked. It creates a loss of the one-to-one relationship that this type of person seeks. He is not so much concerned about failing as about being rejected. In fact, if he fails, but for some reason is still accepted, he feels good. Yet, unfortunately, if he succeeds but for some reason is still rejected, he becomes depressed. The control type is concerned only about losing control, being dependent on someone else, or failing. He does not anguish over what people might say about him so long as they do not block him from gaining his money- and ego-power goals. The ideal: change your attitudes toward failure so that failure and rejection do not bother you while you are in the process of fulfilling your potential. Know that fearing rejection will cause you to become defensive and thus to fail. This knowledge will cause you to reject yourself, and that is good, for if you are not doing what you should be, then you *should* reject yourself. The ideal individual also knows that he often has to lose some control with people if he is going to create the kind of relationship in which he can really win.

Methods

The primary method that the one-to-one type uses to achieve his goal of being liked is to like others as well as to help others—often at the sacrifice of helping himself. This may mean that he achieves goals that satisfy the needs of others but may not satisfy his own needs or fulfill his own potential. The control type of individual achieves his goals of power by always winning. He is very competitive and enjoys difficult situations because he knows that they usually offer greater rewards. He does not particularly care whether other people might lose, and when he is concerned about their feelings, it is only to determine what action to take in order to win. The ideal situation is winning by helping people.

Excessive Stress

When it comes to excessive stress, the one-to-one type will retreat and avoid it; the control type will overreact, venting his anxiety in a volcanic way. The ideal situation is to react, but calmly.

Describing the Opposite Personality

The one-to-one type of individual describes the control type of person as insensitive, crude, obnoxious—a monster. The control type of individual calls the one-to-one type weak, wishy-washy—a mouse. The ideal individual has the ability to identify with all people so that he can work most effectively with anyone.

By reviewing the different ways in which people react based on the types of individuals they are, I am sure that you will better understand who you are. Knowing which type you tend to be should indicate the kind of changes that you should be working on to create more effective balance. Of course you are both people, even though you may have fully developed one side. You may be a control type of person with your children, a one-to-one type with your boss, a control type with new salesmen, and a one-to-one type with your customers. If you are always the same type of person, regardless of whom you are with, then there are going to be times when you have very definite problems. At times when you should be closing, for instance, you may, if you are a one-to-one type, be more concerned about rapport than a decision. Thus, people will like you but you will tend to fail at producing. If you are a control type of person, you may not develop the rapport with your boss, associates, or customers that permits the kind of long-term success you want.

Pecking Order

There is another reason why you may change from one type of individual to another, and this is based on the pecking-order concept. A number of years ago sociologists who went into a chicken yard studied ten chickens and found there was one that could peck all the others but no chicken could peck her. Then there was a second chicken that could peck all the others except the first, and so forth all the way down to the last chicken that could peck no one but was pecked by all the rest. They called this the pecking order, and we find that the pecking order exists among people as well.

You have probably attended a cocktail party or lunched with a few people who did not know one another. Within a matter of seconds one individual was influencing the conversation by determining what the topic would be and directing it as well. Someone else may have tried to say something but was interrupted and eventually silenced by another who may have been jockeying to get into first position. The pecking order is established very quickly, and if an individual is losing and does not mind losing he will tend to become a one-to-one type, at least in this situation. An individual who is not satisfied with that position will become control-oriented. Thus, whenever you find yourself being control-oriented or one-to-one–oriented, you should ask yourself what is occurring at that moment that is motivating you to take on such objectives, what impact you are having on others, and what results you can expect.

What Kind of Relationship?

These concepts of one-to-one versus control not only influence your behavior but determine the kind of people with whom you can work most effectively. To better predict with whom you can work requires that you understand two additional concepts. The first is image matching, which means that you will seek people who are like you. As an example, if you are a control-type of person, you will look for people who are also control-oriented. You will like "winners." The second kind of relationship you will seek is the acceptance of your authority. If you are this control type, you will seek people who are one-to-one types because they will readily accept your authority rather than challenge you.

These concepts can influence you in many ways—for example, the type of spouse you will be motivated to marry will be determined to some extent by whether you are looking for someone who is like you, someone who will accept your authority, or maybe even someone who will dominate you in order to make you feel secure. The individual who wants to be dominated is actually in a third category, which is the subservient type.

If we have a control-oriented individual who seeks a situation in which his authority is accepted and a one-to-one type individual who is looking for someone to depend on, then such people will have a very balanced relationship. This does not mean that it is going to be a healthy one, for what if one person begins to change? The control type of individual may give the one-to-one individual the strength that he or she needs to become control-oriented also. In such a case, the control-oriented individual may feel threatened when his spouse also becomes control-oriented and is no longer dependent. The control type may no longer feel needed and, in order to keep control, may begin using techniques of either rejecting or stifling the one-to-one type. In reverse, the control type who seeks power may have this need for power satisfied by being depended upon—causing the control type to look for a more competitive relationship and thus to drop the one-to-one type.

By knowing the objectives of each of your prospects or customers, of your manager, of your associates, and of your spouse, you will be in a better position to achieve your objectives; for it is knowing what other people seek that allows you to better adapt for both survival and success. At the same time you should not be so sensitive to the reactions of others as to allow them to block you from achieving your goals and fulfilling your own potential.

Sensitivity and Oversensitivity

We know that the major problem people confront is their oversensitivity to the reactions of others. It is not so much the failure experiences in life that might bother you but the criticism from others that you might take personally. It is not the negative comments of others that will cause you to develop a negative self-image *but your assumption that their negative comments are a true reflection of your ability or lack of ability.*

You can improve your self-image and your ability to handle failure if you solve the problem of being oversensitive to the reactions of others and instead react more effectively within yourself. It is not that you should be insensitive to people but that you should not be oversensitive. You know that when you become oversensitive you often have difficulty reacting in a calm, creative way. Instead, you overreact by becoming too apologetic or too aggressive; or you may withdraw, reducing your chances of achieving anything.

Interestingly, most people who appear insensitive are usually oversensitive. They appear not to care because they are so oversensitive that they are afraid to express their feelings. If they are one-to-one types and express their emotion, they might appear foolish and be rejected. If they are control types, they might appear weak and risk losing control. In either case there is a fear that the emotional involvement might cause vulnerability and possibly ego damage.

It is unfortunate that the oversensitive individual so often must insulate himself and thus appear to be insensitive, for his projection of insensitivity can actually lead to rejection or at least a loss of acceptance from others. This will cause even more oversensitivity, causing more ego insulation, less involvement, more negative feedback, and thus a vicious circle.

The initial solution is not to care so much. What if you can reduce your concern about others to a level at which you are sensitive about people without being oversensitive? Then you could express your emotions comfortably and enjoy getting involved as well as reacting in a healthy way to the negative reactions of others. If people react negatively, you will now be able to ask yourself *why* rather than withdrawing into a shell.

The way you react to people is primarily determined by your past experiences. Most people who depended on others in childhood may never have developed a dependence on themselves. Thus they continue to care too much what others say about them. Then there are some people who, in childhood, never depended on others. This can develop when the child is given everything he wants to the point where he believes that the world "owes him a living." In other cases, his parents may always have taken advantage of people and he has identified with them. In reverse, his parents may always have helped people and were taken advantage of, and he decided to go in the other direction. He becomes insensitive to people and does not care.

This individual must develop a value system, believe it important to be interested in the feelings of others—if only to achieve his own objectives. If he continues to see people only as objects, he should at least appreciate the importance of not *projecting* such feelings. Either way, an improved impact on others can lead to the kind of success patterns with people that might actually change his image of himself and his value system. He may begin to gain an appreciation for people that was not developed in childhood.

Test yourself to determine if you tend to be oversensitive, sensitive, or insensitive. In a given situation with someone, are you primarily concerned about helping others, achieving your objective while helping others, or achieving your objective regardless of what happens to others? The objective should be to strive toward the goals that satisfy your needs and fulfill your potential while helping others. You should not be so concerned about the reactions of others that you try to please them at the expense of your own personal development. Equally, you should not be so concerned about yourself that others become hurt.

Ability to Take Criticism

Sensitivity to others can take many forms, such as the ability to take criticism. Most people have a "thing" about accepting criticism, taking it often as rejection. If someone criticizes you—even if it is constructive criticism—it still means they are telling you that you are not as good as you might like to think you are—and that will usually upset you.

Some people appear to take criticism very well but are actually playing a game. Have you ever tried to win acceptance from someone by asking him for criticism? In this way you make the other person feel important, and he will often reciprocate by relating to you. Also, some people know that the best way to stop others from criticizing them is to agree with them. Then there are some people who will criticize themselves in front of others whenever they think they are about to be criticized, because then there is nothing else to be said. They would rather reject themselves than have someone else do it.

Nevertheless, people usually react badly to criticism. They protest or avoid it, thereby losing the benefit of the criticism as well as negatively affecting the individual making the suggestion. True, some people do not know how to criticize. They do so in such a way that it is difficult to accept—heavy-handedly and in magisterial tones that admit no possibility of error. Nevertheless, if you react negatively, you lose the benefit of the criticism—assuming that it has value—and damage your relationship with the individual who is criticizing you. Learning how to handle criticism will have a positive impact on your ability to be sensitive to the reactions of others without being oversensitive.

For this reason set as a positive affirmation the attitude that "I welcome criticism from others."

The second technique to use in achieving this goal is the descriptive technique, in which you describe how you have to act if you are going to be sensitive to the criticism or reflections of others without being oversensitive. The following is a description of how to handle criticism correctly: "Whenever anyone criticizes me, as by saying: 'You dominate people and are too high-pressure,' and I find myself overreacting, I just take the criticism, rephrase it, and then calmly ask them; 'You mean I could be more receptive to people by letting them express themselves more frequently and that I should project more composure and empathy with my present aggressiveness?' "

If you do not achieve this goal, then use the incentive technique and sell yourself on why it is important to you. By accepting criticism I:

1. Gain ideas that can help me fulfill my potential
2. Create a more positive impact on others
3. Learn to be sensitive to the opinions of others

If these techniques do not help you to achieve the objectives, apply the other goal-achieving techniques.

Equally, you should become more effective in giving criticism, and there is a basic technique that you should follow. First determine what you consider to be the individual's basic problem. Try to get beyond his defense mechanism, realizing that the basic problem will usually be a fear of failure or a negative self-image.

Rather than present the problem, you should first ask the individual why he is doing as well as he is. If he is not doing well, the problem may be a negative self-image, and discussing those areas in which he is successful can improve his self-image. Also, the problem is usually not that the individual is wrong but that he is not as right as he could be. The challenge is for him to add to what he is presently doing, but if he is given only bare criticism he may grow discouraged and become even less effective. By discussing his strengths, he will feel more confident—particularly if, once he is finished, you then add a couple more strengths to those he has already mentioned, concluding with the statement: "I have tried to find areas where you can improve and I have been able to find only one. I feel that anyone who has as many strengths as you do should have no problem improving. The only recommendation I can possibly make would be to overcome your fear of failure by doing it."

The Value of Sympathy

Another controversial area when interacting with people is that of sympathy. Control-type people feel that to sympathize with someone who is having difficulty is to justify his failures. As an example, if a child fails at something, sympathy will cause him to feel that the failure was understandable. But in exploring the subject further, we usually find that the control-oriented person is actually more concerned that by sympathizing he may not appear strong but rather weak. If he appears weak, people might think they can take advantage of him; and therefore he may lose control and actually fail. At the same time, the one-to-one type uses sympathy to win acceptance or avoid rejection, claiming that sympathizing is important when someone is hurt physically or psychologically. Which way do you tend to go with the word *sympathy?* It will indicate whether you tend to be a control type or one-to-one type of person.

The solution is again to be found in the right kind of sympathy; and if you follow my next suggestions, it will increase your ability to be sensitive to people without being oversensitive. We know that the fastest way to heal a damaged ego is with sympathy, for sympathy is the opposite of rejection. Once the ego has been healed by sympathy, the individual is prepared for suggestions. He will therefore be ready to try again. Use sympathy as a salve for the wounds of the ego and accept your responsibility to help the individual to try again.

You need people as a way of testing yourself in order to discover how good you are. By competing with them and winning, you prove your own strengths. By helping them, you also gain a sense of your strengths—the kind of positive feedback that improves your own self-image. When you fail, the resultant negative feedback helps you make changes in your course. Often the negative feedback is what you need, for if you are trying to succeed in a situation where most people are security-oriented, you do not want their acceptance. Their rejection may actually indicate that you are succeeding.

Oversensitivity or insensitivity can multiply your problems. For this reason a healthy sensitivity toward the reactions of others is important and a healthy sensitivity to your own reactions is crucial. This becomes one of your major goals, and the achievement of this goal prepares you for the kind of success, self-sufficiency, and self-acceptance that culminates in the personal satisfaction you are seeking. For these reasons, I ask you to make a concerted effort to get totally involved with people without becoming either vulnerable or threatening—helping them while in the process of achieving your own objectives.

In conclusion, you need to be more effective in handling people. This requires that you understand what type of person you are, whom you prefer to deal with, as well as the dynamics of their personality. Whether you are a one-to-one type or a control-oriented individual, you should be familiar with those areas in which you could improve. You also need to react better to people by being less sensitive to their comments to you. This can be achieved by learning how to handle criticism better and by becoming more effective in presenting criticism.

TWO KINDS OF PEOPLE ON VALUES OF SUCCESS	ONE-TO-ONE	CONTROL	IDEAL
When Experiencing Anxiety	Depression	Hostility	Creative Energy
Projects an Image of	Warmth Empathy Sensitivity	Aggressiveness Confidence Strength	Balance
Defense Mechanisms	Nice Guy	Attack	Attack Nicely
Goal in Life	To be Liked	Power Money Ego	Fulfilling of Potential
Methods of Achieving Goals	Liking Helping Pleasing	Winning Manipulating	Winning by Helping Others
Fears	Rejection Not Being Loved	Losing or Being Controlled	Change Attitude Toward Failure and Rejection
When Experiencing Excess Stress	Retreat or Withdrawal	Over Reacts	Reacts Creatively
Describes the Other Individual as a	Monster	Mouse	Identifies with Everyone

XIV

The Psychology of Rapport

That salesmanship is a science is demonstrated by the fact that every aspect of selling can be clearly defined. To begin with, there are two segments to the subject of persuasion. The first consists of the different stages the prospect's mind will go through from disagreement to agreement. You have to realize that in most cases the prospect does not plan to purchase your product. The salesman's objective is to persuade him to do so—and this is not a single decision by the prospect but rather a series of decisions. Understanding these different decisions is your first objective. The second part of salesmanship is understanding the techniques that you can use to identify, from the prospect's decisions, your chance of success or failure as well as how to persuade him to make the right decision!

AIDA

The mental states theory is the oldest and most popular theory in sales use today. The basic premise of this theory is that the prospect's position during the sales presentation can be clearly divided into mental states, specifically the states of attention, interest, desire and action. With this in mind, it becomes necessary for the salesman to develop a series of techniques that will produce these states of mind on the part of the prospect.

The first stage is attention. According to this theory, attention is temporary and must be sustained long enough for the salesman to gain the prospect's interest. Usually attention can be gained by a well-phrased statement, one that is bound to appeal to almost any prospect. In most cold calls, the prospect does not want to be bothered and will give the salesman time to make only one statement. For this reason, an attention-getting phrase must be immediately effective. The salesman must then build the interest into the kind of desire that will prepare him for the final stage of action.

The mental states theory, popularly referred to as the AIDA theory, is basically obsolete, even though it is still used heavily today in many sales programs and texts. This does not mean that it does not work. It is just that there are more effective methods of selling from a conceptual standpoint. It is like the Model T. Ford. It may get you where you want to go, but there are better ways of getting there.

Need-satisfaction Theory

A more recent addition is the need-satisfaction theory. This theory, a result of psychological research, requires that the salesman discover the prospect's needs and make the prospect aware of his needs. The second part, satisfaction, is divided into *satisfy* and *action*. A salesman tries to satisfy the prospect's needs by gaining action.

If we merge these two theories together, we have something more significant. The salesman first gains the attention and interest of the prospect and then discovers the prospect's needs, makes him aware of his needs, and finally creates a desire for the product that culminates in satisfaction.

Series-of-decisions Theory

A third theory in selling is the series-of-decisions theory. It is based on the fact that a sale is not a single sale but a series of sales. If we take our first two theories, the AIDA theory and the need-satisfaction theory, and convert them into a series of decisions, then what are the decisions that the prospect has to make if you are going to make the sale? Try writing down the different decisions the prospect might make—from his first contact with you to the actual purchase—based on the concepts that have already been discussed. How can the word *attention* be converted to a decision on the part of the prospect, and so on throughout each of the stages?

1. Attention: "Do I want to listen to the salesman?"
2. Interest: "Am I interested in what he has to say?"
3. Need: "Do I agree that I have a need?"
4. Desire: "Do I have a desire for what this man is selling?"

5. Satisfy: "Will it really satisfy my needs?"
6. Action: "Is the price right?" "Is the time right?"

Yet recent breakthroughs in human behavior indicate that there are other decisions that a prospect must make before deciding to buy.

The First Decision

If you were to call a prospect you had never spoken to before and asked him, "Are you interested in life insurance at this time?", what response will you receive? Invariably, it would be negative. If a real estate salesman called one hundred homeowners and asked them if they were interested in listing their property in the next six months, perhaps one might say yes; and yet research indicates that at least *ten* of them, on the average, will sell their property in the next six months! Why will so many people "lie" to you? How does this relate to your industry? Of one hundred people, how many—on the average—have a need for your product, and if you ask them, how many would actually respond positively? Why are people so quick to say no, even when they might be interested? It is because people are conditioned to respond negatively to sales messages because of the frequency with which they are exposed to them each day.

The advertising industry is concerned about this sales resistance on the part of the public and does continuous research to determine how many times a person is sold each day. Each time you turn a page of a newspaper you have to decide at a glance what you wish to read; your eye see the ads for a fraction of a second and then tunes them out. How many newspaper ads, billboards, radio and television commercials, and other kinds of persuasive messages do you tune out each day? The advertising industry has determined that you are bombarded by two thousand sales messages per day, and that whenever you suspect you are being sold *you will automatically respond negatively*. It is like Pavlov's dog. Whenever Pavlov fed the dog he also rang a bell. After a while the dog associated the bell with the food and would salivate just from hearing the bell. People are the same. Whenever they suspect they are being sold, they immediately begin to use certain devices they have developed to protect themselves. *Our first objective in selling must be to eliminate the prospect's fear of being threatened in order to disengage his protective devices so he will be receptive to our suggestions.*

Initial Contact

Before you can get the prospect to feel that you are not a threat to him and make him receptive to your suggestions, you must achieve two other objectives. First, you must get him to say no! This is contrary to the traditional view in selling that the salesman should always get the prospect to say yes; yet, if the prospect has a need to protect himself because he is being constantly bombarded with questions that demand a yes, he is going to experience anxiety that he may often take out on the salesman. For this reason, you must let the prospect get this no out of his system by asking a question which allows him to respond negatively. In short, defuse the no!

Therefore your first question, if you are a life insurance agent, is "My name is Art Mortell, and I am a life insurance agent with Prudential Insurance. Are you interested in buying insurance at this time?" The response will probably be negative, and that is good! Your second question: "In that case, is there anyone you know who might be interested in buying life insurance at this time?" Now what have I really asked him? Place yourself in the position of the prospect and ask yourself how you would react to such a question. You will realize that what I really said to him was, "You're off the hook. I'm no longer trying to sell you personally. You're too tough for me." In selling, the words we use often mean something entirely different from their academic definition. We select them more for what they can do than for what they mean. To these words, a prospect reacts as though we had stopped selling him, and thus he begins to relax. We have achieved our first objective: to reduce his fears of being threatened.

Our third question is, "What is your opinion of life insurance?" This question achieves our second objective, which is to convince him that we have stopped selling; we do not appear to be trying to sell him or anyone else at the moment. In addition, this question has many other benefits. It changes his opinion of us, for most people do not believe that salesmen ask questions. If you ask another person about his own feelings, he may no longer see you as a stereotype salesman who is trying to pressure him. Instead he may regard you as someone who takes a personal interest in people even though you are using his opinions to gain an insight into his own buying habits. In addition, it solves the time problem. Up to this point you may have had only a few seconds to deal with, but now you may find yourself with more time than you need! Further, you may have no idea who you are dealing with; but as the prospect answers your question, you get a sense of his personality, such as whether he is particularly aggressive, empathetic, reactive, or reserved. In this way you have an opportunity to gear yourself to his style in order to develop rapport with him.

Most important of all, the third question sets you up for the fourth, which is, "When do you plan on buying insurance in the future?" It is the information that the salesman gathers on this particular question that tells him whom to call back on. In fact, one of the major reasons why salesmen do not do as well as they should is that, as soon as they get a negative response, they back off and often lose prospects that could be gained through greater involvement. For this reason you must make a decision on how many times you should call a potential prospect before you stop trying.

The Advertising Approach

The advertising industry has determined that you should call people approximately five times before you can expect them to buy from you. Of course, this varies extensively from one industry to another. If you are selling magazine subscriptions door-to-door, there may not be enough profit in each sale to justify more than one call per prospect. If you are selling computers, you may make a very large number of calls on the same prospect because of the potential order that is involved. Nevertheless, the average number of calls will be approximately five before the salesman can expect to get the order.

The advertising industry claims that all you should expect to gain on the first contact is the prospect's awareness of you. Again, the problem with most salesmen is that they expect more than is realistic. They often anticipate a sale, or at least an appointment, on the first contact—when all they should expect to gain, in an average situation, is awareness. Because if they actually do sell on the first contact, they use this to justify the premise that they should be able to get the sale on every first contact when, in point of fact, the actual sale was the exception. From this day on, after having made the initial contact, you should ask yourself if the prospect has an awareness of you. If you have gained his awareness, then you have succeeded.

On the second contact, all that can be expected is interest on the part of the prospect. If you are able to get him to agree to accept your literature on the first contact, you have gained his awareness; if reading your literature has inspired some interest, you are still succeeding. You then call him back for your third contact, and your objective is to get him to evaluate your suggestions. If he does this, you have achieved your third objective and are still succeeding. On your fourth contact the key word is *trial:* the prospect tries out the concepts in his mind and compares them to what he may presently be doing or not doing. On your fifth contact the word the advertising industry uses is *adoption.*

To incorporate these five stages into our series-of-decisions approach, the decisions that we try to get the prospect to make are:

1. I am aware that this salesman exists and that he will mail me something.
2. I am interested in what the salesman has to offer.
3. I am evaluating what he has to offer.
4. I would like to try out what he is talking about in order to make a decision.
5. I will adopt what he has proposed.

Your fifth question will vary, depending upon the response you have gained through the first four questions. If the individual appears to be a qualified prospect and reasonably receptive, ask him for an appointment in order to get more involved with him. If he does not appear to be a prospect but was pleasant to speak to, then you would want to get more involved with him because he may be a prospect in the future or may offer you referrals. You would therefore ask, "If I were to send you some literature, would you read it and allow me to call you back and ask your opinion on it?" Or "If I were to send you my card, would you keep it in case you change your plans or might know of someone who might be interested in buying in the future?"

If the individual is not a prospect and was hostile to you, send him a sympathy note as follows: "When I spoke to you the other day, you were rather rude to me. I am sure it was nothing I said, as I spoke to twenty-five people that day and you were the only person who was hostile. I hope whatever was upsetting you has been resolved and you are feeling better. Looking forward to speaking to you in the near future, Sincerely."

Of course, don't send this note without your manager's approval. This particular letter will have many benefits for you. First, you should realize that approximately 20 percent of people are the aggressive, control type who can be very hostile to salesmen. Half of these aggressive people will respect someone who is as aggressive as they are. Therefore, when the salesman responds with this sympathy note or something like it, the prospect respects him for being a "guts ballplayer" like him. The other 80 percent of our population tend to the empathetic type who are often depressed because they are taken advantage of by other people. For this reason they may become hostile with you because they do not know you personally and can take their hostilities out on you without the usual fear of being rejected. When the salesman sends a sympathy note, he often embarrasses the empathetic individual—as he should be embarrassed —for his hostility. In addition, each time you send out this note you remind yourself that *the hostility of the prospect was not personal.*

Most important of all, if we had to determine one reason why salesmen do not succeed, it is that when people irritate them, they do not come back. Surely one of the major characteristics of a successful salesman is that when people are hostile to him, he does react. The challenge is to respond in such a way that you control the situation while still disarming the hostile prospect. Your responses should be primarily empathetic—with some authority in your voice—phrased in question form, and, if possible, with humor. In fact, it would be valuable if you and your associates were to make a list of objections that people might make to you that could irritate you; and then, taking them one at a time, compete for the best reaction. The first person to respond scores a point just for coming back quickly, a second point if it is in question form, a third point if it is empathetic, and a fourth point if it is humorous. Then see who can score the most points. It is important that you condition yourself for success, and the ability to react in a disarming way is an area where you definitely need success patterns.

How Do You Project?

Once you have eliminated the prospect's fear of being threatened so that he will stop protecting himself and become receptive to your suggestions, you are then ready for his second major decision which is "Can I feel comfortable with this salesman?" This question can be answered by the prospect only after he is asked two more important questions. What do you think they are?

Sensitivity

The first question that a person immediately asks himself on his first contact with you is, "Is he sensitive to me?" In order to appreciate the importance of this question, I would like to refer you to probably the most dramatic study ever conducted in industrial psychology. In 1925, industrial psychologists went into the Hawthorne plant of Western Electric in order to determine how much they could increase production by improving working conditions. They improved the lighting, and production immediately increased. With each further improvement in working conditions, there was a corresponding increase in production. Convinced they had proved their point and in order to make sure the study was scientific, the psychologists began to reduce working conditions to observe the degree to which production would decline. But production didn't decline—it continued to climb! Stunned, the psychologists probed for the answer and finally discovered that the reason the women continued to increase production, regardless of whether working conditions improved or deteriorated, was that they felt *someone cared about them*. Each day they would see these executives studying them with stop watches, *paying attention to them*. These are the most powerful words we have in the English vocabulary, that someone is sensitive, concerned, relates, is interested, or appreciates you.

How effective are you in helping people feel that you are sensitive and emotionally concerned about them? If people suspect you are not sensitive to them, they are going to conclude that what you are going to sell them is for *your* benefit, not theirs. Therefore, the question "Are you sensitive to me?" has a dynamic impact; for unless the prospect answers this question positively, there is often little value in continuing the sales process.

The next question is basically the opposite of the previous one, and yet it is also positive. The question is, "Can I have confidence in this man?" The prospect is very concerned about whether the salesman he is dealing with is an authority he can depend on, someone in whose competence he can have faith. What are you doing that gives people the feeling that you are an authority who can help them?

The reason these questions tend to be the opposite of each other is that the type of salesman who exhibits sensitivity usually projects a warm, personable style that is quite at odds with the aggressive, confident type of salesman who radiates authority. Of course, the challenge is to balance both of these personality characteristics so that people feel you are not only *concerned about them* but are *capable of helping them*.

Body Language

How do you create that kind of impact on people? There are three elements that create your overall impact on people, and the first is words. Latest research indicates that words make up only 7 percent of this impact. Tone of voice represents 35 percent of the impression. Just to dramatize the difference in importance between words and tone of voice, you can call a person a "son of a . . ." in many ways. The tone of your voice can indicate either love or hate. The other 58 percent is based on body language, such as facial expression and the movement of the hands as well as the entire body. A person leaning forward with his hands extended indicates that he wishes to express himself. A person leaning back indicates that he is being receptive. A person with his arms folded and a friendly expression indicates that he is receptive, and with a frown indicates that he is defensive. A person telegraphs most of his feelings through nonverbal communication.

Within this area of image projection, your objective is to balance opposite characteristics of personality in such a way that anyone can identify with you. This is the definition of *charisma*. When you think of any field of human relations, such as selling, the ministry, or politics, you will find that those who are most successful are those who have developed nearly every characteristic of personality and blended them together into a well-balanced projection. A good example of charisma would be Jack Kennedy, who balanced seriousness with humor, aggressiveness with sympathy, composure with enthusiasm, strength with warmth, and confidence with receptiveness. What characteristics should you be developing that will help you to be more effective?

Some people fear that in developing new characteristics they may lose their present strengths. Yet without certain characteristics, the individual already suffers an imbalance within his personality that reduces his positive impact on others. It is similar to beef stew. Regardless of how good the beef is, if you leave out the potatoes, it isn't beef stew. A proper blending of all ingredients, far from detracting from any one ingredient, enhances all of them. To project a "new" characteristic does not mean you will be insincere, for all characteristics are potentially within you. They are not "new." I am sure you have tried developing all of them but have had some bad experiences with a few of them and thus have avoided using them. Someone may have reacted negatively when you tried using a particular characteristic such as enthusiasm, confidence, or humor; and thereafter you believed that this quality was not within your personality. Rather, you have just not used the characteristic often enough to blend it into your personality, and that is the challenge to you at this time.

Attention Span

Once you have allowed the prospect to relax with you, assured him that you are concerned about him and that you are an authority that he can depend on, you are ready for the next step of the sales process, the attention span. You must be sensitive to the amount of attention you generate. If you are selling in a retail store and someone comes to your counter, you automatically have a few minutes of his attention, since he already has some interest. If you are calling someone on the phone regarding life insurance, you may have only a few seconds of his attention. Once you have gained attention, it does not mean that you disregard this area. You may be able to move on to your next objective within the sales process, but you must continue to keep his attention.

Acceptance Span

Throughout the entire sales process you must also be very sensitive to the acceptance span of the prospect. In other words, what is his span of acceptance, or how quickly can he make a decision? As an example, how long will it take someone to decide if he can relax with you? If he is from the South, he will probably relax more quickly than someone who is from New York City.

If you push the individual to accept too much at one time, you will threaten him and he will begin to protect himself; and yet if you reduce your efforts you may not accomplish as much as possible. When a stockbroker proposes fifty shares of stock at $60 per share, how will the prospect react? How will he accept it? If he is not at this purchasing level, he will feel that the stockbroker is too sophisticated for him. However, if he is usually buying 100 shares at $100 per share, he may feel the broker is below his level. The broker has not been selling according to the customer's acceptance but on the acceptance within his own image. Nearly all persuaders are guilty of this. The life insurance salesman also allows his own image to get in his way. He will try selling a $10,000 policy to a man who will only buy $5,000 and also to a man who wants $50,000. In different ways he will lose in each situation.

The problem is that you too often base your selling on your own worth rather then the prospect's. The parent and teacher often do the same in setting goals and limitations for the child, basing them on their own opinion of what he should achieve. You have to be sensitive to what the individual can accept and how it relates to what you want him to accept. How comfortable must he feel about you before he is ready for you to discuss his needs or problems? Again, it varies from one prospect to another based on the acceptance-span concept. You have to be prepared to make a greater effort with one prospect than another in order to gain his attention, his confidence, or to complete any other stage in the persuasion process.

If you are successful to this point in eliminating the prospect's fear of being threatened, in assuring him that you are sensitive to him, projecting that you are an authority in whom he can have confidence, developing the attention span and in knowing what his acceptance span will be throughout the sales process, then you have completed the first of the four major stages within this persuasion process. The one word that best symbolizes the overall objective in this first stage is *rapport*. You are striving to establish a relationship in which the individual will be receptive to your suggestions. There is a basic formula, that the sensitivity of what you wish to discuss with the prospect is determined by the depth of rapport that you have established. As you establish greater rapport, you will be able to become more involved with the prospect so as to better achieve each stage of the persuasion process.

XV

Consumer Motivation

Once you have established rapport you are ready for the second stage, which is consumer motivation. You cannot expect to persuade anyone to your way of thinking until you know what they need and want as well as why they may not want to agree with your ideas. Therefore you must know what motivates the prospect and what demotivates him. In other words, what his needs and his antineeds are. From another viewpoint, the prospect has many needs, and if they are important to him and they are not satisfied, they develop into problems.

In order to discover what motivates the prospect, the salesman must become proficient at asking questions. As an example, in the real estate industry the salesman will ask such questions as, "How many rooms do you need?" "How much do you feel you can afford?" "Do you want much landscaping?" "What kind of area are you interested in?" "How many bedrooms do you need?" "Do you want a pool?" Armed with this information, the broker obtains a selection of homes that meet the general requirements of the prospect. In viewing the homes, the prospect is turned off by most of them but becomes excited by one in particular. The odds are that this home has the same basic features as most of the others—yet there is something about this home that interests him. What is a home buyer really looking for?

Before answering this question, let us examine the stockbroker-age industry. Why do people buy stocks? Mainly for the sake of financial security or, more pointedly, to satisfy their greed. Everyone knows that! But as we examine this concept more closely, we discover that people will invest for reasons other than financial return. When I was a salesman in New York City, I learned that the discussion of stocks at a cocktail party was "in." "What are you in now?" If you did not have stock, you did not "belong" to the group. We also find that the primary motive is often pure gambling. What kind of stock people buy is another facet. Exactly what does determine why one prospect will buy mutual funds, another growth stocks, and still another speculative stocks?

The prospective home buyer is looking for a home that is an extension of his image of himself—more importantly, one that represents the kind of image he would *like* to have of himself. The same applies to almost every product we purchase today. The person buys the kind of stock that represents his image of himself. If he sees himself as the kind of person who is trying to get rich quickly, he will tend to buy speculative stock; if he sees himself as a stable, mature individual who is slowly but consistently growing, he will tend to buy growth stocks. If he sees himself as already successful and wants to protect what he has established, he will lean toward blue-chip stocks. Probably the best example of buying based on self-image rather than need is the purchase of a car. Cars are available in an infinite number of choices. Chevrolet alone has more than forty models, and when you consider all the color combinations available, you end up with a huge selection just within this particular model.

You can do a reasonably good job of analyzing people just from the kind of car they drive, and, more significantly, from the kind of car they prefer to drive. The car they are presently driving will indicate the image they had of themselves in the past when they purchased the car or the image they have of themselves presently. The kind of car they would prefer to drive will indicate the image they have of themselves at this time or the image they would like to have of themselves if they had nothing blocking them. If the car you are presently driving is basically the same kind of a car you prefer to drive, *you are basically satisfied with the position you have reached in life*. If there is a major difference between the kind of car you are driving and the kind of car you prefer to drive, it indicates that *you are dissatisfied with your present level of achievement*.

The first factor in analyzing personality is the type of car—station wagon, compact, sports car, or sedan. A sedan indicates that the individual tends to be stable, mature, and rather satisfied with his present level of achievement. The sports car indicates that the individual is anxious to grow and has not yet reached his expectations. The compact indicates that he is security- or economy-oriented, whether he would like to be or not. A station wagon indicates that he is family-oriented and is more interested in recreation than in business.

The next factor is color. Red and yellow are the aggressive, "breaking loose" colors. Red is group-oriented in the sense that the individual likes to break loose *with* people, while yellow may be chosen by the self-sufficient individual who likes to break loose on his own. White is optimistic, while black is conservative. Brown or bronze is the professional or businesslike image. Green is stylish and mod, while blue is pleasant and comfortable. Gold and silver both project the image of success, but gold tends to be people-oriented, silver very self-sufficient or individualistic. The deepness of the color or the amount of yellow added determines how subtle or obvious the individual wishes to be. A dark green indicates that he wishes to be stylish in a quiet way, while the adding of yellow to the green indicates an aggressiveness toward being fashionable. Add yellow to red and you get orange—and a greater orientation toward breaking loose; while if you darken the red you get a more subdued aggressiveness.

The manufacturer of the car also is a major factor. In the European car we have a status orientation but in an antistatus way: the individual does not want to be classified as a conformist by American middle-class standards. He wishes to be unique and therefore is oriented to the foreign car. A General Motors product indicates that the individual is outgoing and aggressive; the Ford indicates a more practical orientation; the Chrysler is similar, with a conservative approach; and the American Motors car indicates a security orientation. In fact, the American Motors car indicates an "underdog" association.

The model indicates the individual's image of himself financially. In General Motors products, we find the Chevrolet projecting an image of $8,000 to $12,000 per year; the Pontiac, $12,000 to $18,000; the Oldsmobile, between $18,000 and $25,000; the Buick, $25,000 and up with a professional image; and the Cadillac, $25,-000 and up with an aggressive image.

There are many other factors as well: A convertible indicates breaking loose while a vinyl top indicates breaking loose in a more subtle way. Another example is the color of the interior. Imagine a black Lincoln Continental and the image it projects. Now, would your opinion change if the interior was red? True, a person may also drive a certain car to create a false impression: the doctor might drive a VW to convince his patients he is not really after their money. But the individual who is motivated to purchase cars in order to please others rather than himself reveals something very definite about his personality.

To better dramatize the importance of the product's image within consumer motivation, examine automobile advertisements in magazines. In the Camaro or Mustang advertisements, you see young people who do not appear to be married traveling in open country. For more expensive sports cars like the Firebird, Cougar, or Cutlass, young people who appear married are viewed in such activities as sailing or tennis. They are still active—but in a more establishment-oriented way. Of course, in station wagon ads you see such activity as shopping or preparing for a vacation with the family. With the Cadillac we observe people in formal dress entering a Colonial mansion for what appears to be a lively party. In the Lincoln Continental advertisements, a mature man stands beside the car with a lawn sweeping back behind him to trees in the distance that partially hide a Tudor mansion. Each of the advertisements is saying to you, "Isn't this what you are after?" or "This is the way you want to be."

Again, the importance of image matching and consumer motivation applies to virtually every product category. For example, a particular cigarette brand will usually be purchased because of image matching. What image do you think a cigarette like Salem or Newport is trying to sell when you see a young couple in a rowboat just floating on a pond that reflects the green of the surrounding trees and meadowland? In fact, you can hardly see them smoking, because the cigarette is secondary to what they are trying to sell you. The green symbolizes fertility, the young couple symbolize youth, and the pond indicates comfort. They wish to convince you that if you smoke their brand of cigarette, all these things will come to you. What are they selling in the Marlboro advertisement in which you see the rugged man out on his own, making it by himself and obviously independent? If you want to be self-sufficient, then you will want to smoke Marlboro. At the same time, Virginia Slims and Eve appeal to the need that women have to show their independence. One way to help a person stop smoking might be to reverse brands, such as asking a woman to smoke Marlboro or a man to smoke Virginia Slims.

Regardless of whether the product is cigarettes, automobiles, stocks, computers, insurance, or real estate, the way the product's image relates to what the consumer seeks is a crucial factor in persuasion. Do these concepts relate to your product? If a product is developed properly, it should project an image that will capture a significant portion of the market. You should know which particular part of the market your product is best suited for based on image matching. Otherwise you may be wasting your energies with prospects who believe your product is not suited for them. If you know which part of the market identifies with your product, then you will know where to focus your efforts.

These same concepts in image matching that influence a prospect's purchasing decisions also determine his attitude toward you. People have to "buy you" as the kind of person they want to be involved with, and this requires that you project the kind of image that they can identify with. Look at yourself: your hairstyle, your clothing, the sound of your voice, your facial expression, the car you drive, whether you smoke or not, the words you use, and the subjects that you are interested in discussing. This should help you to realize the overall image you project to people. Now, are you projecting the kind of image that will assure your success within the market in which you are presently involved?

What Does the Product Promise?

What you are really selling is a promise. People buy not only the product but also what the product promises to do for them. The real estate investment salesman has to decide why the individual will be buying land and then he must *promise* something. He will promise that the land will offer security, will fight inflation, will be a long-term investment for retirement, will make him rich, or is a gamble that he should win. Consider the buying of soap for 20 cents and buying cleansing cream for $2. Since both are for cleansing, why does one command ten times the price? The difference again lies in a single word, a *promise*. Soap promises to make you clean, but cleansing cream promises to make you beautiful! Each projects an image that promises something different, and each is purchased (and priced) accordingly.

The Problem in Determining Needs

When you begin to probe in order to discover what might really motivate the individual, you are going to be blocked by any number of possible obstacles. As an example, in a study by the Color Research Institute, a group of women were given three boxes of detergents to test. They believed that the first detergent was too weak and in some cases left their clothing dirty. The second was too strong, and they claimed that it actually ruined some of their clothing. The third was just right. As you may have guessed, all three boxes contained the same detergent. Why were the responses different? It was the color of the package that stimulated the different responses. The detergent that was "too weak" was in a blue box, the one that was "too strong" was in a yellow box, and the detergent that was supposed to be just right was in a blue box with yellow splashings.

Since this study was conducted a number of years ago, adjustments have been added to washing machines and fabrics have become stronger. For this reason the market has switched to stronger detergents—and you now find a variety of detergent boxes exploding in yellows and oranges to signify strength.

Another reason why people may not be honest is dramatized in a consumer research study of beer preferences among men. The question asked was, "Do you prefer a light or regular beer?" The preference was light, three to one. This presented a problem for the beer manufacturer who had the test conducted, since he was producing nine times more regular beer than light to meet the needs of the market. Why did people respond so differently? Light was preferred because the word symbolized the distinctive and sophisticated, while the regular symbolized the common and ordinary. If asked what they preferred, the answer was "Of course, light." But when asked what they drank, the answer was "I buy the regular because it gets me there the fastest for less money." You may ask people what they prefer, but that may have little relationship to what they will actually purchase. People often tell you what they think you want to hear, as well as what they want to hear themselves say, but their more basic and motivating needs are often quite different.

The salesman is often wrong when he makes assumptions about what will motivate the consumer. Toothpaste is just such an example. For years it was assumed that people used toothpaste to keep their teeth clean and in order to avoid tooth decay and cavities. As reported by Vance Packard in *The Hidden Persuaders,* a test was conducted to determine the most popular time of the day to brush your teeth. It was found that a major percentage of people brushed their teeth in the morning before breakfast and in some cases would not brush again until the next morning. This is actually the worst time of the day to brush your teeth, for it is just after you have spent the longest period of time accumulating food particles and just before you start putting them back in again. For this reason, the toothpaste manufacturers had to realize that people were actually brushing for a different reason: to have a healthy, clean-tasting mouth as they started the day and before eating. With this information, they introduced a new brand, Gleem with GL 70. The GL probably stood for guilt, and it went to second place with a very effective slogan. What was the slogan that motivated so many people to buy?

That most people do not realize how much they are influenced by advertising at the subconscious level is proved by the fact that they purchase products without realizing the techniques that were used to persuade them. Millions who were influenced by the Gleem slogan would not be able to recall what the slogan was. Why? Because we have been conditioned below the conscious mind. And yet we will recognize it quickly once we hear it: "Gleem is for people who are too busy to brush after every meal."

As you realize the difficulty that exists in determining the true feelings of people, you must set an objective to establish the kind of relationship that allows for an honest exchange of ideas. You do not have the right to discuss a prospect's needs or problems until the relationship is established. Even then you cannot expect honest answers. You cannot assume. You must consider every possibility, and become more involved in order to gather as much information as possible.

Prospect Must Understand His Needs

Once you discover what the needs and problems are, both mechanically and psychologically, what do you do next? Most salesmen believe this is the time to present solutions, but often this will create a gap within this persuasion process. You may have discovered what the prospect's needs and problems are—but does he consciously *know* what they are? For this reason the next stage is to show him what his needs are.

As difficult as it may have been to discover what the prospect's needs are, it is often more difficult to get the prospect to agree what his needs or problems might be. Frequently, he may not even wish to admit this to himself. It is important that you understand what may be causing this difficulty as well as how to resolve it.

Most people cling to inertia like a security blanket. When they are going in one particular direction they are in balance; but if someone suggests another approach, then they have a conflict. This triggers frustration and anxiety, resulting in depression or hostility. If the prospect is unable to express his hostility, he will become depressed; either way he will avoid your suggestions in order to keep himself comfortable.

Disturbing the Prospect

At the same time you, as the persuader, have a specific responsibility if you sincerely believe that the prospect should be making a change, and that is to destroy his state of equilibrium by disturbing him about his problem. In trying to persuade a homeowner to list his house at a more reasonable price, you often have to confront him with the facts, such as the value of his home, directly. In trying to persuade a parent that he needs insurance, you often have to make him acutely aware of his responsibilities. In persuading a decision maker to purchase, you may have to disturb him about the problems that will exist if he does not keep up with his competition.

Often the prospect may be disturbed about his responsibility; but what will happen if you are reluctant to disturb him for fear that you will be rejected? You may avoid "telling it like it is" and lose the sale, as well as wasting your time. Further, you have failed the prospect, for you have not improved his position; and he may subsequently buy from a salesman who *does* impress him with the nature of his problem. Then you will really be rejected. And you should be.

When motivating others, whether selling prospects, associates, friends, or relatives, you begin pleasantly and positively. At the same time, if you sincerely believe you have a responsibility to help the individual and he is not being honest with himself, you have to increase the pressure. You have to begin to disturb him if you are going to break through his defense mechanisms in order to help him to understand his responsibility to his family, his business, or himself.

XVI

The Psychology of Persuasion

Once you have established rapport, discovered the prospect's needs and problems, and made him aware of them, you are ready for the third stage. There are two parts to this stage. One is to present the solution to the problem. The other is to realize that people have many needs, but to get them to make a decision requires that you convert their needs into desires so they will not be happy until they have what you are recommending.

From an ethical view we must be careful to help the prospect, but not to the point that he overextends himself. Due to the influence of Madison Avenue, a large part of our population is suffering from overstress because they believe they must have various luxuries in order to be happy. At the same time, most people do not earn the kind of money that will allow them to afford these luxuries. This creates a conflict that establishes real frustration and anxiety within them.

FABR

In presenting solutions to the prospect, you should follow a formula of four steps. First you list the features of your product or service. You must realize that people never buy features per se but rather the concept of what these features can do for them. If cars

169

were just for transportation, there would be a very small selection of cars; but because of status and image matching, the concept of what a car will do for the consumer takes on a far more significant impact. For this reason, you must convert the features (F) into advantages (A) and the advantages into benefits (B) that the prospect will appreciate; and then you can ask for a response (R).

As an example, if I were selling my workshop seminar, I would take one of the features of my program and present it in these four steps: "My seminar features closed circuit television. The advantage to you is that you will see and hear yourself as others do, leading to the benefit of a greater sense of self-awareness and increased sales. Isn't that what you want? If the prospect agrees with one of your FABRs with enthusiasm, he is telling you it is time to try closing.

Overcoming Objections

If he comes back at you with an objection, this should please you; for as long as he has objections and you do not know what they are, you are blocked from the sale. For this reason, you should welcome objections, because the sooner you discover what they are the sooner you can overcome them. At the same time, you must realize that most salesmen are afraid to ask for a response because they take objections personally. Again, we cannot be so sensitive to the reactions of others as to lose control of the situation.

Give some thought to why you may tend to present only the features and not the advantages and benefits. Is it because you think in terms of *your* product and *your* interest rather than the prospect's needs and problems? Give some thought to why you may not be asking for a response. Is it because you are afraid of rejection?

Satisfaction

Your fourth and last major stage is satisfaction. Again, the word has two parts, *satisfy* and *action*. If you satisfy people in the sense that you are pleasant, discuss their problems, and present ideas that can help them, they will be pleased and comfortable with you. In this way you have gained acceptance, but what about action?

Satisfy without *action* means a lack of financial success to you and an indecisiveness on the part of the prospect that can also hurt him. In other words, if you do a fine job in your presentation but do not decisively try for action, your prospect will be satisfied in the sense that he feels comfortable with you and is pleased with this new awareness of his problems and available solutions. Yet the prospect's satisfaction must be based on solving his problem by taking action. This requires him to make a decision that will improve his position.

Many people look toward you, the salesman, for that decisiveness. They assume that you know what they need and what is available. If you do not persuade them to buy, they assume you do not yet know what they should be purchasing. They do not realize that the reason you are not asking them to make a decision is that you are afraid of being rejected by them. If this continues, they may eventually buy elsewhere; and then you will feel rejected. Help them make a decision so they can solve their problems and get on with the other affairs of their life. Otherwise your desire to please and be accepted causes you to become indecisive, and you therefore fail and feel rejected. Just as an advertisement should sell a product rather than be remembered as a pretty advertisement, so should you fulfill your responsibility by not being just another "nice guy" but by helping people make decisions that culminate in satisfaction.

This concept of satisfaction applies just as well to our relations with our children. If we are afraid of being too decisive with our children and having them reject us, we may fail in our responsibility to help them become successful. Worse, they may look toward others for a source of direction, often with unfortunate results. If, in selling, you are not decisive, your prospect may look for another salesman.

Yet you are right in not wanting to be so decisive as to threaten the prospect and risk losing the all-important rapport. How do you achieve action without losing the prospect? You do it carefully by using the right techniques.

How to Close

You know you have to close about five times before you can expect the order. If you know what techniques to use, the prospect will always be comfortable. You do not try closing until you have gained a positive response from one of your FABRs, which is your signal that it is time for a trial close. As an example, if you are selling a $25,000 insurance policy and the prospect responds positively to one of your suggestions, you should come back and ask him, "If you like that, why don't you buy a $100,000 policy?" Make sure you smile and say it with humor, and watch his response. If he says, "How much more would that cost?" he is probably interested in more than $25,000 and you should seriously pursue the $100,000 policy, or at least more than the $25,000 policy. You do this by answering his question of what it would cost and ask him how he feels about owning a $100,000 policy. If he tends to be negative, you might try coming down to $75,000 or $50,000.

What does it mean if he says: "I can afford only this policy?" It means that he is ready to buy, and you should ask for the order. "In that case, would you give me your signature here?" If he says, "I'm not even sure I can afford this policy," you may have more selling to do. If he says, "I can't even afford this policy," you do have more selling to do—or you should be selling him a policy that is less expensive. If you believe that he really needs this particular product, you had better determine the objection.

Overcoming Closing Objections

First of all, you have to find out if the objection he is giving you is the actual objection or a device to protect himself from having to make a decision. How do you find out? You rephrase his objection in question form. As an example, if he says, "I am not even sure I can afford this policy," come back at him with the question, "You can't afford this policy?" or even more subtly, "Afford this policy?" What are you doing in such a technique? You are asking him to explain in more detail what he has said.

Frequently the prospect will give you an entirely different objection because your technique has gotten through his defense mechanisms and elicited an honest response. If he goes on to explain to you why he feels the way he does—such as not being able to afford your product—it usually indicates that his objection is sincere. He might, for example, come back and tell you that he cannot afford to make the initial payment for thirty days. *Now you know the objection you need to overcome.*

Remember, you love hearing objections, because as long as they are hidden, they are blocking you from the sale. The sooner you can find out what they are, the sooner you can overcome them. With the last objection you might be able to come back and tell him, "There is no problem. You can buy now and make a payment within thirty days if that is all that is blocking you from purchasing at this time." If the answer is positive, he has purchased. If he comes back with a negative response, such as, "Well, let me think about it and call me back tomorrow morning," you will have to try again. Your ideal question at this time is, "I guess there are still some doubts in your mind. Could you at least tell me what might be bothering you?"

Three Kinds of Responses

There are actually three responses you can get from a prospect in a closing situation. The first is agreement, in the sense that he accepts one of your suggestions or your answer to an objection of his. In such case, *assume his consent and ask for the order.* The fact that you are asking for the order and assuming he is going to buy is aggressive on your part. If your style is empathetic he will not feel threatened. Again, we are merging the best qualities of our one-to-one and control types of salesmen.

If he tries to stall you without a specific objection, probe by asking questions that assume there is something concerning him. If you believe he has doubts or objections and for some reason does not want to tell you, use your empathy aggressively by explaining: "Up to this point I felt you were with me. Now it seems something is bothering you and yet you don't want to tell me." You phrase the statement in question form, lean back, and wait for a response.

To repeat: If you are given an objection, play back the objection in question form. If the prospect claims, "I need more time," you just rephrase the objection as a question: "More time?" As soon as you feel you have reached the real objection, you have the responsibility to overcome it directly or to point out other benefits that compensate for what might be a legitimate objection. With these techniques, you can go through many closings without threatening the prospect—while at the same time increasing your chances for the order and the prospect's chances of satisfaction.

Criteria Selling

If you know the prospect is interested in buying but plans to consider a competitive product, you need to apply criteria selling. This means you set criteria or standards for what the prospect should be looking for in a product. Then, when he does consider a competitive product, there is a greater chance he will judge it with the standards *you have set*. The basic approach is to explain those features he should look for that are crucial for his satisfaction and to list those features that tend to be unique about your product. Then, if he fails to find them in the competitive product, he will have a greater tendency to return to you. Your chances of success in a competitive situation will be much stronger if you have done a thorough job in all the previous stages.

In conclusion, appreciate the fact that persuasion is a science in which you go through a series of very specific stages. If, in the future, you find yourself having difficulty, take it for granted that you have skipped one of the stages or have not attained the one you are presently trying to achieve. Also realize that while you may know what you should be doing, there might be specific reasons why you may not act. You may not want to project emotional concern about the prospect if you are a control type of salesman who tends to be afraid that such a display may cause the prospect to think you are weak and can be taken advantage of. If you are a one-to-one type of salesman, you will be reluctant to project authority and confidence for fear of threatening the prospect and having him reject you. If you are a control type of salesman, you may have difficulty asking questions in order to discover the prospect's needs. Rather, you will tend to assume you know what his problems are and proceed to tell him how to solve them. If you are a one-to-one type of salesman, you may spend too much time developing rapport and discovering needs but avoid presenting solutions for fear he may object to you. If you are a control type of salesman, you will tend to present solutions rapidly but may not ask how he feels about your suggestions for fear he might challenge your position. If you are a one-to-one type of salesman, you will do a fine job of satisfying the prospect in terms of pleasant conversation, but you may be reluctant to close and gain action for fear of rejection. If you are a control type of salesman, you may close too early and too hard and not give the prospect the feeling you are trying to satisfy his needs. For this reason, if he does purchase, he may quickly experience "buyer's remorse"—and the sale could later be canceled!

Although you may consider these the greatest selling ideas in the world, if you are afraid to lose control or afraid of rejection you may be reluctant to use them. The control type of salesman has to learn that often the best way to win is by giving up yardage. If you yield control temporarily by asking a question, you may gain the kind of information about the prospect that allows you really to control the situation. You often have to withdraw in order to score, as the football quarterback retreats under the rush—only to fire a "screen pass" into weakly defended territory. If you are a one-to-one type of salesman, you must realize that the best way to gain the acceptance of the prospect is through his satisfaction, which requires an aggressiveness on your part. It is through a happy customer that you will gain the kind of referrals and acceptance that you are seeking. It is easy to sell people, but not so easy to sell yourself on selling people. Before you can start motivating others you will have to begin to motivate yourself. Persuasion begins from within. That is your responsibility.

XVII

Techniques of Persuasion

Once you understand the objectives of the sales process, you need techniques not only to achieve the objectives but also to help you identify what stage you are at with the prospect. How do you know whether you have gained sufficient rapport or whether you need more? How do you gain rapport? These same questions apply to every stage of the persuasion process.

Image Projection

The first techniques are those of image projection; i.e., by projecting certain characteristics you convince the prospect you are emotionally concerned about him, and this will help you to establish rapport. What characteristics? The keynote characteristics would be warmth, friendliness, and sensitivity. If you plan to use humor, this would be the appropriate time, if you can produce a light, personable projection. With these qualities you will put the prospect at ease and help him to feel that your primary interest is helping him.

With the rapport established, what characteristics do you think should now be projected within the need-problem stage? The major ones are sympathy, receptiveness, and concern. With the projection of these characteristics, you show a concern for the prospect's problems and an interest in listening to what he has to say. This encourages him to express his feelings.

At this point, you should give some consideration to your ability to change projection. Do you have the ability to move from a pleasant, warm approach to one of receptiveness and concern? Might you be reluctant to project certain qualities? Possibly you have tried some and failed—humor, perhaps—or know of someone who was, say, sympathetic and was often taken advantage of. Maybe you tried enthusiasm or aggressiveness and had people reject you for "coming on too strong." Regardless of the reason, you should know why you are not as effective as you should be. At least be honest with yourself and then decide how much you can change.

The third stage requires the projection of competence if you hope to be effective in presenting solutions. If you expect to develop needs into desires, you must also project enthusiasm. But the need to project both enthusiasm and competence at the same time can cause a conflict. To project competence requires a serious, analytical, deliberate approach, which usually gains agreement. Yet, for a lack of enthusiasm, the agreement may not culminate in an actual sale. Enthusiasm, which requires the expression of emotions and excitement, may gain the order; but the next day the individual may question why he bought it. He may have difficulty thinking of logical reasons for his behavior and decide to cancel. Which way do you tend to go? Do you become very serious and competent, or very quick and enthusiastic?

In our last stage, which is satisfaction, you must project sincerity in order to satisfy the prospect and conviction in order to gain action. The balanced projection of sincere conviction should help you gain the right decision for the prospect and your own success as well.

Territorial Infringement

Another approach to techniques of persuasion requires a familiarity with the concept of territorial infringement. Each individual has his own territory and resents any encroachment. As an example, if you go into an elevator and someone is standing on one side, you will stand on the other side. It is automatic, and yet to do otherwise would be very uncomfortable. Imagine an airline terminal with fifty seats and only one person sitting on the front left side. How might he react if you sat beside him? Have you ever been on a New York subway during rush hour when the train stalls under the East River, the temperature is 85 degrees, the humidity is 90 percent, and you are squeezed against many people? No one says a word or looks at anyone else. To do so might indicate there was something wrong with him.

Each individual needs a territory. Deprived of a physical territory (elbow room), people withdraw within themselves and become psychologically isolated. When this occurs, they cannot become involved with others, nor can others become involved with them. *Whenever you enter an individual's territory which includes his property, home, office, or telephone, you threaten him and trigger his defense mechanisms.* Again, one of your major abilities with people, particularly in selling, should be to enter their territory without threatening them. This requires practice, such as starting conversations in an elevator or on the street. Each day you are presented with opportunities to practice territorial-infringement techniques, such as moving your chair around an executive's desk when presenting material to him. Of course, all these techniques should be practiced only in unimportant circumstances until you are reasonably sure of the dynamics involved.

Your ability to resolve fears of failure and rejection, as well as your sensitivity to the types of people with whom you are dealing and your skill in projecting the appropriate image, will help you become effective in territorial-infringement techniques. Now for a discussion of these techniques.

Hypnosis in Selling

Is it possible to hypnotize the prospect in order to increase your chances of persuading him? In a rather interesting way, it is very possible. In fact, it is being done constantly in advertising because, as discussed previously, *hypnosis* is only another word for suggestion. Any technique that causes an individual to be receptive to your suggestions is a hypnotic technique.

Watch how hypnosis or suggestion is used in advertising. First, your attention is gained through such methods as humor, excitement, beauty, action, or color. The hypnotist or the salesman will use enthusiasm, humor, body language, and facial expression to gain attention. You too want the prospect to focus all his thoughts on you. Otherwise you are competing with thoughts that may distract him from your suggestions.

It is important to the individual not to feel threatened by your emotional expressiveness; therefore your impact must have a significant degree of empathy. You must cause him to concentrate all his thoughts on you. Many persuaders do this by threatening and attacking, but this is dangerous because it builds a quiet resentment that can culminate in a real loss for everyone. Empathy and emotional concern must be merged with your attention-getting impact techniques to assure him that what you say will be for his benefit.

A third element needed is authority. You must project qualities of strength and confidence so the prospect can feel secure with you and allow himself to believe what you have to say. You must be careful not to threaten him by attempting to get this attention too quickly; the projection of strength must be calm but firm. This is what a doctor projects when he "sells" you on the operation.

Now you have caused him to focus all his thoughts on you. You are an authority, and he believes and feels you are concerned about him. You are ready for the next part, which is to relax him. This is crucial, for as long as he feels anxiety he will defend himself and resist total involvement with you. He will also have difficulty making decisions for fear he might make the wrong decision. If you can relax him to the extent that he feels no need to protect himself, he will be more receptive to your suggestions.

To achieve these four objectives, in that order, requires you to change your projection from a quick expressiveness to a softer, more relaxed projection, inducing him to become comfortable and receptive. In doing so you should gradually develop a pleasant monotone, focus on his eyes without intensity, and use words that make him feel secure and relaxed.

Switching from enthusiasm to a pleasant, calm projection must be done gradually or the prospect will become distracted and thus defensive, which destroys your objective. Therefore, the change in projection must be gradual. After you achieve these objectives, you are ready for the final part, which is to make the suggestion to him. This should be done with a strong projection of authority as you state: "And I strongly recommend you make this decision at this time for your benefit."

Pecking-order Techniques

How does the pecking order relate to you? When you become involved with people, are you usually able to control the situation? Do you find yourself involved but unable to control? Or do you find yourself trying to become involved but being interrupted?

If you are a one-to-one type who does not want to dominate people, you may not be as successful as you would like to be. You may find you are too anxious for pleasant relations, allowing others to control the situation and block you from attaining your objectives. You need to learn how to control in order to succeed, which does not mean you become an aggressive, high-pressure steamroller. All you need are those techniques that allow you to capitalize on your existing strengths.

If you are a control type of salesman who threatens people, you may win the battle but lose the sale. In other words, you may control the prospect but lose the order. You need to use techniques that allow you to control while disarming people.

Capitalize on Small Victories

The first concept is that winning in the pecking order does not require a wide marging of victory. In sports it is often considered poor taste to win by a very wide margin and humiliate the other team. The same applies to the pecking order. If you can gain a slight edge, you are in control. At this point you should capitalize on your position and seek agreement, allowing the other individual to agree without losing self-respect rather than overwhelming him.

If you begin to gain a very strong position, you will often trigger resentment and the individual will seek ways of thwarting you. If he is afraid you might attack him, he may use very subtle techniques that might be difficult to recognize, such as avoiding you when you need a response, being critical of you to others, or lying to you. If you had capitalized on your small margin of victory or control and not gone for the overkill, you could have gained agreement without triggering resentment. Whether you win by one point or a hundred, you still win; but by how *much* can you win before people resent you and strive to get back at you? Learn to be satisfied with a small margin and then capitalize!

How to Take the Initiative

What approach should you take when you initially become involved with people, whether one person or a group? Should you speak first and try for immediate control? Yes and no. You should open first in order to demonstrate that you have more initiative than anyone else, but you should not try to control. Your only interest at this point should be to determine the other individual's position. In other words, you are gathering information that will tell you where agreement exists, where there is a difference of opinion, where there are weaknesses in the prospect's viewpoint, how you might be able to gain control, what type of personality he has, how to gain rapport, and what you need to do to succeed. How can you possibly expect to achieve your objectives, regardless of what they might be, if you have not gained this kind of information?

There is another objective, and this is to show the prospect that you are interested in his viewpoint—and you are. By demonstrating an interest in him, you gain the kind of rapport that will help him to relax and answer your questions without being defensive.

If you wait too long before expressing your opinion, you risk creating an impression of indecisiveness that will discourage people from accepting you as an authority. If you seize the initiative and express your views in such a way as to gain control, you may win the game of "king of the hill" but also encourage others to gang up on you. You may find yourself losing or getting a cold shoulder from the group. Worse, they may let you control so they can understand all the things about *you* that you should be determining about *them,* and this may assure your defeat. To sum up: You want to express yourself as soon as possible, but only for the purpose of gathering information.

The classic method of getting people to express themselves is by asking open-ended questions. An open-ended question is a question that cannot be answered positively or negatively but only in opinion form; for example, "How do you feel about life insurance?" "What is your opinion of investing in stocks?" Or, "What are your views on computer applications within your industry?"

Look at all the benefits derived by asking open-ended questions:

1. You determine the prospect's needs and problems.
2. You determine his personality and what you must project in order to create rapport.
3. You demonstrate an interest in him which takes you beyond the stereotype of the salesman who does not care.
4. You determine areas of agreement and possible disagreement as well as areas where agreement might be easily attained.
5. It gives you enough time to develop your next move rather than quickly moving from one comment to another.
6. You relax the individual because you are allowing him to control and you are not threatening him.
7. You expand the attention span because as long as he is talking, your time is not reduced. The open-ended question actually increases time as the prospect thinks to himself, "If you are willing to listen to me for five minutes, I should at least give you a couple of minutes in return."

While there are many benefits to an open-ended question, the prospect should not suspect that, by presenting his position, he is helping you to control him. If he does come to believe this, you have a problem. The test of whether your open-ended question is gaining results or hurting your position is simply the response. Is the prospect becoming more responsive or more defensive?

Express Response

Regardless of your results with the open-ended question, you can do better with the "express-response" technique. You express your point of view and ask him an open-ended question of how he feels about what you have said. You never explain so much that, if he disagrees with your ideas, you cannot reestablish agreement. At the same time, you must say enough to encourage him to express his feelings. This is the unique benefit of the express-response technique: as the prospect thinks to himself, "If you, the salesman, are willing to tell me how you feel, I should be willing to express my viewpoints to you." For example, you might say, "I believe the right kind of insurance should be good protection and a good investment, and there are many kinds of insurance programs to meet the needs of each individual. What is your opinion?"

Sentence Completion

One of the most sophisticated techniques is the sentence-completion technique in which you allow yourself to be interrupted in order to gain many of the benefits of the open-ended question. Think about the times people have interrupted you. As irritating as it might have been, you have to admit it allowed you to determine the individual's true feelings. If you give some thought to the way you verbalize your ideas, particulary at what point you pause as well as the inflection of your voice, you will realize there are times when you actually encourage people to interrupt you. You do this, for instance, when you finish your thoughts with "and. . . ."

Since your objective is to determine the true feelings of the prospect on specific subjects, your approach is to begin speaking on the subject without really saying anything definite and pausing frequently, particularly in the middle of a sentence. For example, "I don't know what your views are on investing . . . (pause), but it is really serious when you realize what a small percentage of our population is financially independent at the age of sixty-five . . . , particularly when there are so many ways to invest. . . . I don't know what your opinions are . . . , but . . . there are so many approaches . . . to solving this problem." With the right inflection and properly placed pauses, you will invariably be interrupted and gain the kind of spontaneous response you need in order to determine your prospect's true feelings on the subject. Since people would never suspect you wanted to be interrupted, they will tend to respond spontaneously and openly.

Seek Attack

The "seek-attack" technique is even more subtle, since you present your views so as to encourage attack. People never suspect someone wants to be attacked; therefore they respond quickly and honestly. The way you seek attack is to attack, which, of course, will initially have a negative effect on the rapport you may have developed. This problem is solved by attacking lightly and—with empathy—criticizing your prospect's position on some subject of little significance.

You do this to determine his position in a particular area that may hold the key to his overall feelings. Don't be surprised if he agrees with you. But if he disagrees with you, then agree with *him*. This may increase the rapport to an even greater extent. Such an approach might be as follows: "I think your existing program is insufficient because it does not resolve this specific problem."

Of course, outright attack is never recommended since all that can be expected in return is resentment or counterattack. Whenever you attack someone, he will look for an opportunity to get back at you, such as uniting with others against you. People who tend to be aggressive are most comfortable when they are attacking and, unfortunately, they often do not realize the antagonisms they are causing.

Agree, Explain, and Add

The most effective technique is agreement. "You are right . . ." and continue by explaining "The reason you are right is . . ." You explain why your ideas are both compatible and complementary to his ideas. Most people are rendered defenseless by this approach; they can attack when provoked, but not when you defuse them with agreement. If you first agree and then add your point, the prospect will have difficulty challenging you. Make sure that you do not say, "Yes, but . . ." or "Yes, however. . . ." This indicates you have said yes only in order to disagree. When you tell a prospect why you actually agree with him, he assumes you are objective as well as sensitive to him. This will cause him to be receptive to your thoughts. Now for a number of other techniques for gaining agreement.

Praise

Whenever you have the opportunity, you should offer praise. You know the greatest motivator is self-acceptance and the most effective way to help an individual gain self-acceptance is to appreciate him. In praising, you improve rapport and encourage him to become more expressive.

Sympathy

Another method of encouraging expression is sympathy. When a prospect has a problem that blocks and frustrates him, he needs someone who can sympathize with him. He needs to feel that someone understands his situation, and your expression of emotional concern will do just that.

Reassurance

Another method of gaining involvement is through reassurance. When the prospect expresses fears or doubts, you should not be too quick to skim over these feelings but rather explore his uncertainty and reassure him. In some cases you may know the prospect's doubts do not warrant serious thought. Nevertheless, the expression of doubts, small as they may appear to you, may be of real importance to him. They may not even reflect what is actually troubling him but may represent something else entirely. He may either be unaware of his real problem or he may not feel comfortable enough with you to express it. Either way, through reassurance and patience on your part, you can not only gain greater rapport but learn as well whether the fears may be taken at face value or whether they are symbolic of something else.

Giving of Yourself

A fourth technique, which is actually a common denominator of most techniques of persuasion, is "giving of yourself." The golden rule teaches us to "Do unto others as you would wish them to do unto you." Yet we still hear people say, "Do unto others before they do you in." The first idea is correct. How can you expect people to give of themselves if you are reluctant to express your own feelings? Tell people how you feel, express your own thoughts and emotions, and people will usually begin to do the same. Nevertheless, you cannot assume they will express themselves. For this reason, you must often ask the individual to respond.

Encouraging Expression

Another technique for encouraging expression is to repeat what the individual has said. Done properly, it demonstrates that you are following his thoughts and are interested in what he is saying. This will often encourage him to be more expressive.

Reflective Questions

Another questioning technique is reflective questioning. It has two major applications. The first one is often too effective. For example, "If I can show you how you can sell your house for the price you want and do so more conveniently, would you list your house with me?" The technique is excellent because the person will have a natural tendency to answer yes. We then gain agreement on a number of secondary points which, added together, represent the overall benefit. We assume consent: "You agreed that you would let me sell your house if I could prove why it is to your benefit. Since you have agreed to these basic points which prove I can do the best job for you, I assume you are ready to list your home with me."

Too many people sense what is coming when they are asked the first question: "If I can show you . . . would you . . . ?" Instead, they defend themselves: "I don't know what you are getting at . . . but no." *All techniques become distracting and discrediting if they are obvious.* Each technique you use should be subtle and woven into your presentation in a way that does not tip your hand. These techniques must be well timed, properly phrased, and properly blended together. Another way you can use this technique without threatening people is to ask for a reasonable decision such as, "If I could show you a way of increasing your office production by 50 percent, would you allow me to make a presentation of our new product line, read my literature, or give me fifteen minutes to discuss it in more detail?"

A second application for reflective questions, discussed in the previous chapter, is in determining the nature of the objections you are confronting. One of the greatest frustrations for the persuader is to meet objections and not know if they are legitimate or contrived to get rid of you. The reflective question can help you determine the truth. Regardless of the objection (e.g., "I cannot afford it"), we take the objection and rephrase it, "Oh, you feel you cannot afford it?" Now watch the impact of the question. What you are really asking is: "I am not sure I really understand. Could you explain yourself in more detail?" With this approach, you often find the prospect explaining: "Well, actually the reason I feel I cannot make a decision at this time. . . ."

In this case you will find you are dealing with a defensive objection, one that is meant to protect the prospect from you and your suggestions. Why do people actually lie so quickly? As discussed, we are bombarded by two thousand sales messages each day, and when we suspect someone is trying to sell us, we immediately defend ourselves. Threatened, the prospect will offer the first objection that comes to mind. A true objection is referred to as an attitude objection. In this case, at least you know where you stand and can prepare to change the prospect's thoughts.

The third type of objection is the prejudice objection. This arises when the prospect is unequivocally opposed to what you are presenting. We have medical doctors who are prejudiced against chiropractors, psychologists who are prejudiced against psychiatrists, liberals who are prejudiced against conservatives, and vice versa. When someone says, "I don't believe in life insurance" and gets up on the table and starts yelling, this tells you something. You are probably wasting your time, and you should go on to someone who may offer a greater opportunity.

Direct Questions

Your third and last questioning technique is a direct question where you are looking for a yes or no answer. Persuaders have a tendency to use this question too frequently rather than encourage greater expression through open questioning. Nevertheless, the direct question is valuable in presenting solutions or giving a demonstration. This was discussed in the previous chapter on presenting solutions based on the FABR concept. You present the feature, the advantage, and the benefit. Then you ask for a response by asking a direct question such as "Does that sound reasonable?" Or "Don't you agree?" At this point in the sales process, having gained the rapport and the information necessary, you are looking for a definite response in order to determine if the prospect is ready to buy or if there are still objections to be resolved. Your closing techniques are also direct questions, such as, "If you have no other objections, are you ready to buy?"

Coalition

If you are having difficulty and all techniques seem to be failing, my last suggestion is to create a coalition with someone like the prospect's spouse or business partner. This is how you can win at a cocktail party or at a sales meeting when someone is dominating in the pecking order. By creating a coalition you can gain control and win.

The techniques you use are primarily determined by the stage of the persuasion process. Just as you project certain personality characteristics in order to gain rapport, discover needs and problems, present solutions, overcome objections, and close, there are specific techniques to use within each one of these stages. When establishing rapport and gathering information, you want to emphasize open-ended questions. Sentence-completion techniques help to gather information. When presenting solutions, you use direct questions. When overcoming objections, you use reflective questions. When closing, you use direct questions.

The last concepts under techniques of persuasion are *persistence* and the *willingness to fail*. Contradictory? Not at all. You should develop a repertoire of techniques to allow you to gradually move toward the sale without coming on so strong at any one point as to threaten. If you are afraid to fail, you will not use them. In the pecking order we find that the individual who believes himself worthy of winning will be persistent. If he fails, he will determine why, modify his course, and try again. It is with this attitude that these techniques of persuasion will prove amazingly effective for you as well!

XVIII

Leadership

We have discussed—and, we hope, improved—your ability to persuade others; but there is an additional dimension in this challenging and fascinating field of selling that is also important: leadership. If you are going to capitalize fully on your potential, you must be prepared to lead others. This relates to every aspect of your life: family, community, or business. By taking on the responsibility of leading others, you are better able to reach new levels of personal success. By helping others to be successful, you develop and demonstrate your own ability.

You cannot expect to enjoy the growth of your own children if you are not prepared to meet the responsibilities involved. You cannot expect to gain the ego satisfaction and financial rewards of being an executive if you are not ready to shoulder the problems of others. Yet how can you expect to lead others if you are not ready to lead yourself? Leadership must begin *from within.*

Leading yourself starts with an objective awareness of yourself. To illustrate: whenever you join a group, whether at a cocktail party or on a new job, what are you most concerned about? It is probably the need to be accepted. And this need motivates you to adapt or conform to the group even though you sacrifice your own objectives in order to belong. This can cause you to compromise your own self-interest, abandon your potential, and shelve your other needs. All to be accepted!

For this reason it is crucial that you be very careful about the kind of group you are adapting to. If you are at a party, does this mean you must drink? If in a sales group, does this mean that instead of prospecting, you must play golf or pool? If there is the danger of adapting to the wrong kind of group, you should either solve the problem of needing the acceptance of others or make sure you join the right group.

Yet who determines the nature of the group? Not so much each member of the group but a specific type or types of individuals. If you know what kind of individual determines the nature of the group as well as what each member must do in order to be accepted, you can follow a new and more effective path. Rather than conform and risk sacrificing your objectives (or holding to your own objectives and risk ostracism by the group), you might want to consider an alternative. If you were to take the role of leadership and influence the group in terms of what its objectives *should* be, you would gain a new level of personal development. You could then involve yourself with any group, because you would not be influenced negatively. In addition, you would exert a positive influence on the group which would enhance your opportunity for achievement. You would also gain the benefit of testing yourself and deciding whether you would like further leadership responsibility, as in management.

Who wouldn't want this kind of responsibility and the success it would bring? You, perhaps? Are you afraid of failing, or is it that you might not see yourself as *belonging* in that kind of position? Why might you be afraid to fail? Is it a fear of rejection? Why might you be so sensitive regarding the opinions of others? If you do not see yourself in a position of leadership, why not? Is it merely because you have never been a leader before?

Are you even sure you want to be a manager? The Peter Principle states that "People rise to their level of incompetence," and the way to avoid the problem is to avoid being promoted. For this reason, it is important to understand what to expect when moving into management so you will be both prepared and also certain that you really want to meet the challenge of management responsibilities.

Who Is a Manager?

First of all, what is the role of a manager? A manager is usually considered to be someone who helps people set and achieve goals, who motivates them and attends to their problems so they can better utilize their ability.

How many salesmen can a manager motivate and help without spreading himself too thin? The figure depends on a number of factors—such as the complexity of the product line and the seniority of the salesmen—but we will use eight as an example. Imagine that we have a manager who is effective with eight salesmen. Either he or his company may now want him to expand to nine salesmen. While the ninth man may not present a serious problem, the manager may soon find himself with a tenth man, and that may turn out to be the straw mat that causes the manager to rise to his level of incompetence. The manager is incompetent to handle that large a crew. Equally, the company may instead be concerned about the development of high producers and potential managers. Yet as long as the salesman depends on his manager, he will have difficulty becoming a high producer or becoming qualified for management.

The point I am stressing is that a manager's major role is managing people in such a way that they can manage themselves and do not need him. If a manager can help his salesmen become self-sufficient, he can effectively go beyond the original eight. He can hire more salesmen and create better training programs. Further, he is in a stronger position to help salesmen reach their full potential as well as to prepare them for management.

Why Are You Successful?

This presents two challenges. Initially a manager, if he is to build successful, self-sufficient people, must understand why he is successful and self-sufficient. First, if you have to be a manager, you must be a successful salesman—which means you will be technically competent as well as competent in sales ability. Now it is true you can train people to acquire technical and sales skills, but what about the challenge of training people to be self-motivated? Does the successful manager even know why he is self-motivated? In review of the text's material, there are five reasons why an individual will be self-sufficient:

1. He has the ability to fail and continue trying.
2. He has the ability to come back at people who threaten him, but in a disarming way.
3. He enjoys converting anxiety into creative energy.
4. He is able to change his self-image, attitudes, and habits.
5. He enjoys—and is committed to—continuous growth and achievement.

How to Develop Others

If you are achieving these five goals to a significant degree, you should be seeking new challenges. Knowing *why* you are successful qualifies you to help others develop these same abilities so they can also become self-sufficient. Therefore the second part is knowing how to help others develop their abilities. You should also understand the reasons why you may have difficulty helping salesmen become self-sufficient.

To succeed in management requires the same abilities as succeeding in sales. Nevertheless there are reasons why "people rise to their level of incompetence," and one is because the manager often loses some of his previous abilities or does not use them as extensively as he should.

Ability to Fail

We have seen that the major ability of the successful salesman is that he can fail and continue trying. If people reject him on the phone, refuse to buy when he tries to close, or cancel their purchase afterwards and yet he perseveres, he will usually succeed. Again, *people usually fail in selling not because of the many times they have failed but because of the few times they have succeeded.*

If you can handle rejection and come back, you *will* succeed. If you want to continue progressing, you will want to move into management. At this next level the rejection is usually more ego damaging. This is due to a basic principle: the greater your emotional involvement, the more sensitive you are to the possibility of failure or rejection. A prospect's opinion that your product is worthless is not as upsetting as a potential recruit's opinion that the sales manager's work is worthless. If you make a sales presentation and the prospect begins to object, it is still not as threatening as when a salesman objects to a manager in a sales meeting. While it may be disappointing to lose a customer, it is more depressing to lose a salesman whom you have tried to help for a lengthy period of time. If the salesman has the ability to fail and continues trying, he will succeed; but can he handle the deeper failure and rejection a manager experiences without taking it so personally as to want to quit?

As long as you can endure failure without discouragement, you will stay on the straight road to achievement; but at the point that experiences of failure begin to irritate you, you will look for a detour: avoidance. At which point of involvement does your objective switch from achievement to avoiding failure? Does the fear of failure deter you before you have achieved your expectations? What do you need to do in order to strengthen your ability to persevere so you can enjoy continuous growth and achievement?

Defense Mechanisms

Now for the second challenge, which involves strengths and defenses. In chess, football, or war, it is important that you have not only the strengths required for victory but also the defenses that are needed in the event of attack. If you overemphasize defense, you will lack the strike capability to move forward. You may not lose, but neither will you win. And if you are not achieving your objectives, whether it be in football, a battle, selling, or managing, you are losing!

With the right kinds of strengths and defenses, you may succeed in selling; but if you move into management and you feel threatened, you may no longer capitalize on your strengths and instead have to call in the defense to save you. Defenses reduce the chances of people "getting to you" but also lower your chances of success because you are insulating yourself from the kind of involvement you need with people. Being too aggressive can threaten them. Being too much the nice guy can cause a loss of authority and results.

There *are* certain defense techniques that are appropriate in selling, such as the humility defense. Here you "psyche out" the prospect by maintaining a low profile: play yourself down and play up the prospect. In this way, you make him feel important and reduce his feeling of being threatened. He relaxes, becomes receptive to your suggestions—and you strike! This kind of defense can score in selling but will have a damaging effect on the manager's image as an authority. The humility defense can cause him to appear weak. Thus tactics that can help you win at one level can often cause problems at the next; it depends on the opposition.

In fact, the ability to play the right kind of game is often the reason salesmen are promoted. But the problem that all too often occurs is that while the salesman's game playing might win success, he may, in becoming a manager, play games in order to avoid failure. As a salesman, games helped him win; as a manager, games help him to avoid failure. For example, he may use his defenses to avoid making decisions. He tries for the tie and loses.

Strengths

In a similar way, the salesman's strengths can become his defense if he now feels threatened in his new position. One of his major strengths may have been enthusiasm, coupled with receptivity to the prospect's objections. If, as a manager, he is afraid of failure, he may be unable to cope with the salesman's objections. Now he may use his enthusiasm as a defense by presenting his suggestions with such fervor that his salesmen never have the opportunity to object. In this way he does not feel threatened but neither does he determine the salesmen's objections. Thus they might be dissuaded from following his suggestions.

Equally, strengths that make wine for a salesman can turn into vinegar at the next level. There are many such examples, such as the fact that the successful salesman is usually very good with people and concepts but has little patience with paperwork and details. In management he needs to be good at both, and if he does not develop the necessary management skills, he may rise to his level of incompetence.

A successful salesman might lack the needed management strengths not through a lack of ability or a lack of interest but because of a negative self-image. He does not see himself performing certain management functions, such as detailed paperwork. And, while the salesman may see himself as the successful manager, he must also have the right attitudes and habits. You can have a positive self-image, but if you do not change your habits you are not going to gain the success patterns you need in order to justify your new self-image.

Anxiety

Another challenge relates to anxiety. Increased responsibilities at the management level offer increased opportunities to fail as well, together with an increase in anxiety. If you can handle the anxiety at one level, can you handle it at the management level?

A specific reason why, in your new position, you may have dif- difficulty as a salesman. As an example, the development of rapport not take out your anxiety on the customer. You were therefore forced to discover creative ways of eliminating anxiety. But as a manager, you no longer find yourself in a subservient position and can take out your anxiety on your sales force. Thus, your ability to convert anxiety into creative energy may be lost.

The difficulty in moving from salesman to manager relates not only to such subjects as handling failure and anxiety and changing self-image, but also to the ability to persuade. Obviously a salesman must have the ability to sell, but, not so obviously, a manager requires even more of this same ability. This is because *it is easier to sell a prospect on why he should buy a product than it is to sell an individual on selling it.*

Persuasion

The first part of a sales process is developing rapport. How much rapport do you need before you can start asking questions of a prospect? As a life insurance salesman, how much rapport do you need before you can ask a man how much his wife would need if he should die? How much rapport do you need before you can ask a prospect in real estate how much he makes per year in order to determine what kind of house he can afford? On a scale of zero to ten, you might need a rapport of five or six. To be successful in selling requires that you not only be effective in developing this amount of rapport but also be able to move on quickly to discovering needs.

Rapport

If you do not develop enough rapport, you will not get honest answers or the person may avoid you by asking you to leave or by withdrawing into nonresponse. Spend too *much* time in developing rapport and you may never get involved enough with your product to be really effective in selling. Therefore, the successful salesman has the ability not only to develop a rapport of five or six but also to move on quickly to the problems and needs of the prospect.

As a sales manager, how much rapport do you need before you can ask a man why he is an alcoholic, why he is depressed, why he refuses to prospect or close or why he tends to be hostile with his associates? You need a great deal more rapport than five or six before a man is willing to answer such questions. If the salesman has conditioned himself to move quickly to a rapport of five or six and then move into the sales presentations, he may become incompetent as a manager if he never develops more than a five or six in rapport with his salesmen. He never gains the kind of relationship or enough understanding of his people to present solutions that they will accept.

There are other areas within the subject of rapport that can also present a problem to a manager who may previously have had no difficulty as a salesman. As an example, the development of rapport requires two major factors. The first is that the individual feels you are emotionally concerned about him, as we discussed in the Hawthorne studies. Otherwise he is not going to answer your questions or accept your suggestions.

As a manager, you have to realize that a salesman's problems are usually more complex than those of a prospect. For this reason you need a far greater degree of rapport than you need with a prospect. In the field you had to be understanding, because the prospect was the boss. Now, as manager, you may no longer see yourself as the person who has to please but rather as the boss who is supposed to be pleased by the salesmen.

The manager may also feel that the kind of emotional concern I am talking about may cause him to appear too sympathetic. His salesmen may then think him weak and take advantage of him, and he might therefore lose control. If control is what he wants, he may then avoid projecting those characteristics that would cause him to lose control with his people. By maintaining his authority image, he may control in the sense that they do not challenge him; but in turn he may lose, for if they feel he does not care about them, they will not follow his suggestions.

Authority

The second factor that determines the development of rapport is your projection of strength and authority. As a salesman, it is important that the prospect believe in you; but at the management level this becomes crucial. To your salespeople, you must be the Rock of Gibraltar, someone they can *depend* on in times of stress. Can you project the kind of authority that will cause salespeople to assume that you are someone who can help them when they find themselves in trouble?

There is a reason why some people do not want to appear authoritative. They are concerned that the projection of such characteristics as aggressiveness, confidence, and strength may threaten people, which may result in a loss of acceptance. If you avoid projecting such characteristics, it is true you will not threaten people, but it is equally true you will not gain the respect you need in order to be accepted as an authority. In the final analysis, you may get what you feared—rejection.

Attention Span

Another aspect in developing rapport is attention. A salesman knows the importance of attention and works very hard to gain it. But a manager often does not like to think he has to gain the attention of his people. As manager, he assumes they will pay attention to him as a matter of course.

Yet, gaining a prospect's attention requires that you say things that make him feel that he is going to benefit from your comments or presentation, and this is of even greater importance in the manager-salesman relationship. The salesman is really not going to pay attention unless he feels that the manager is going to say something that will benefit him. If the manager's suggestions are only for his own benefit, he will have difficulty gaining the salesman's attention. The salesman has the same difficulty when he tells the prospect things that appear to benefit *him* and not the prospect. In such a case the prospect tunes out the salesman and might ask him to leave. If the manager talks for his own benefit, the salesman will also tune him out. He can't leave, because his job would be jeopardized, so he will appear to be interested. Thus, the manager who believes that as an authority he does not have to ask for feedback may lose the salesman's attention without realizing it. He has wasted his time giving suggestions and reduced his own as well as his salesmen's effectiveness.

Acceptance Span

Another factor in developing rapport, as well as every aspect of persuasion, is the acceptance-span concept. A salesman knows it takes a certain amount of time to develop rapport, to gain attention, or to complete any other stage of the persuasion process. For this reason, he paces his presentation to a speed the prospect can handle. Yet, as a manager, he may feel everybody should travel at the same speed he can. If he is good at closing, *everybody* should be good at closing. If he excels at prospecting, he tends to become impatient with the salesman who has trouble "hacking it." He is reluctant to travel at the salesman's speed. For this reason, one of the major abilities he may have had as a salesman—to understand how quickly a prospect can make a decision—may now be lost as a manager.

I am not suggesting that a sales manager should move slowly, but before you can get a train to move quickly, you first have to get on the train. You cannot expect the salesman to move quickly until you first get on his train of thought and begin moving initially at his speeds. This concept applies to any relationship—handling your children, your prospects, your salesmen, or anyone with whom you become involved.

Need/Problem

The second major stage of persuasion involves the need or the problem. As a salesman you have to discover the needs or problems of the prospect, and invariably they are of a technical nature. There are also psychological needs, such as the fact that the program you are presenting must project an image that is compatible with the prospect's self-image.

While the prospect's need or problems may not be that easy to discover, the needs or problems of a salesman are far more complicated. A successful salesman has the ability to determine the needs and problems of a prospect quickly, and this skill might propel him into a manager's chair. Here he will be required to discover the psychological needs and problems of a salesman, such as why the salesman may have a drinking problem, why he may come to the office discouraged in the morning, why he may be afraid to prospect and close, why he may level off at $1,000 a month, or why he may be hostile when given suggestions. He forgets one thing: he himself was successful because he either had no serious problems or spontaneously reacted positively to them, and now he can't understand the kinds of problems *most* salesmen experience! If he hopes to be successful in management, he has got to realize he is different from *most* people. He has got to be able to stop stretching and cutting them to fit *his* measuring table. No, it's not easy. Most of us use ourselves as a measure in passing judgment on others. We can't understand people who don't think as we do. As an example, the manager will state that successful salesmen are primarily money motivated. This is not true.

Even if the manager does determine what the salesman's needs and problems are, he may have difficulty getting the salesman to understand what they are. Far easier for a salesman to get a prospect to realize his needs and problems than for a manager to get a salesman to realize his. One reason is that a salesman has to tread very carefully so he will not threaten the prospect. As manager, he might see little need for treading carefully with his salesmen because he's the boss! In "telling it like it is" the manager may threaten the salesman and cause him to become defensive and unreceptive. The point that we keep coming back to is that the persuasive ability of the salesman might be lost when he becomes a manager for a variety of reasons, such as the fact that by seeing himself in a position of authority he begins to feel he no longer needs to use the same subtle techniques of persuasion. Another reason is that he may feel comfortable recommending technical solutions to a prospect but he may feel he is not a psychologist and therefore feel very uneasy about working with his people at a personal level.

Problem Disturbance

We know that if the prospect does not agree with our analysis of his needs and problems, we have failed unless we disturb him. If we really "get to him," he may have no choice but to face up to the facts we have presented. The reason why the successful salesman, who is now a manager, may not want to disturb his salesmen is that he feels by threatening them he may damage morale within his sales force. As a salesman he was often willing—even eager—to take a chance on disturbing a prospect, because all he could lose was a sale. As a manager he may feel he cannot afford to lose a salesman and therefore may never disturb them. Thus, sadly, he never helps them to achieve their objectives—or his own.

Desire/Solutions

The third major stage in the persuasion process is presenting solutions to the individual's problems. This must be done in such a way that his needs are converted into a desire, which motivates him to follow the solutions. In the persuasion process, the successful salesman makes a real effort to sell the prospect on his solutions. He converts his product into a series of features, advantages, and benefits and then asks for a response.

As a manager, he may have difficulty understanding why he *has* to sell his people on what they should be doing. Therefore, when he presents solutions, he may just say, "I was a sucessful salesman and that's why I am a manager. This is why I succeeded as a salesman, and this is what you are going to do to succeed as a salesman. Therefore, you do it this way." He does not break down the specifics of what he is asking them to do. He just tells them what to do. He does not convert his thoughts into advantages or benefits (as he did when he was a salesman), and therefore he loses the sale! He has failed to sell the salesmen on his suggestions. The manager has not motivated them as he once motivated prospects; he has lost one of his major sales abilities.

Further, he may not bother to ask for the salesman's response, for this might imply that he is not really in control. As a control-oriented salesman, he may have tempered his aggressiveness with subtle techniques that helped him to achieve his objectives; but as a manager he no longer sees the need for them *and therefore loses one of the persuasive strengths that originally justified his promotion!*

Another difficulty that can develop within this third stage relates to overcoming objections. A successful salesman welcomes objections because he knows that as long as they exist, they block him from succeeding. He needs this negative feedback in order to make corrections in his course. But now, looking down from his new perch, he may see objections from a salesman as an indication that he is losing control or as a challenge to his position. He therefore will use certain techniques calculated to discourage the salesman from presenting objections. The salesman refrains from disagreeing, and the manager never learns the salesman has any objection. Both of them lose.

Satisfaction

The last stage of the persuasion process is creating satisfaction, which again has two parts: satisfying and action. The control type of salesman knows that he has to achieve more than just action if he is going to avoid "buyer's remorse" and will therefore make an effort to use pleasant, subtle techniques in order to satisfy the customer while gaining the order. As a manager, he may have difficulty understanding why he has to work so hard to satisfy his salesmen.

He feels his job is to tell· them what to do and "I don't care how you do it!" His salesmen can't help feeling that only *his* needs count. Result—damaged morale and "salesman's remorse."

The one-to-one type of salesman works hard to capitalize on his sympathetic style and gain the order, but as a manager he may get so emotionally involved with his people as to be afraid to be decisive for fear they might reject him. For this reason he continues to be very emotionally concerned and sensitive, but he may not be decisive because there is too much at stake! He is reluctant to "close" on the salesman; the salesman may not be able to accept him as a leader, and therefore rejects him. So he works hard to satisfy his salesmen but never really creates the kind of action that can assure their success as well as his.

In review, the characteristics that are needed to succeed as a salesman are the same characteristics that are needed to succeed as a manager. Yet, for a variety of reasons, the successful salesman may not continue to use all of his strengths as a manager and therefore may "rise to his level of incompetence." As a salesman, there are a number of specific benefits that you can derive from an appreciation of the *causes* of the manager's difficulty. First of all, it might help you decide whether you'd want to consider management. Further, you might be more sensitive to the difficulty your manager is experiencing; by understanding, you will be in a better position to relate to him. The manager-salesman relationship has to be based on two-way communication, as in any relationship. There is no reason why the salesman cannot play a more significant role, just as a child should play a more significant role with a parent. If you, the salesman, feel dissatisfied for some reason and have come to better understand, through this material, *why* you are dissatisfied, then you have a responsibility to your manager to help him to understand where the breakdown is occurring. If you use effective persuasive techniques in communicating your concerns to him, it should prepare both of you for far greater personal benefits. Just as leadership begins from within, so too must you often take the initiative, regardless of your position within the relationship.

XIX

It Is Your Responsibility

History displays a disturbing pattern; the rise and fall of civilizations in a rhythmic cycle that seem as consistent as the tides. Sometimes the tides rise more quickly, sometimes not as high as at other times; but they always rise, then fall. So it is with nations. It is the influence of the moon and sun that determine the flow of the ocean. So too are there forces that influence the rise and fall of nations; but these forces are not as clearly defined.

Equally, the weather can often influence the tides. A strong wind against the ocean can retard the power of a rising surf, just as a storm at sea can cause the waves to pound and rip away at a fragile coastline. In a similar way you can watch forces retard the growth of a nation; some nations will sweep over others when driven from behind by a more aggressive people.

While there is a similarity between the rise and fall of the tides and of nations, there is one marked difference. The tides are primarily influenced by external factors, while civilizations usually grow and die from within. Outside influences can destroy a nation politically, militarily, and economically; yet if its people survive psychologically, the nation will soon begin to grow—often reaching new levels of power. The growth and achievement of Germany and Japan after World War II are just such examples.

Surely it would be invaluable to understand these factors that convert a primitive people into a dominant civilization; for such knowledge could be applied to all institutions within a nation. It could have a dynamic impact on the family and the raising of children, education, the training of business people, and the development of political policy.

While any one of many nations could be studied in the search for these factors, my initial choice is Portugal. In 1215, the Portuguese defeated the Moors and gained their independence, almost three hundred years before Spain.

But the challenge to be free had created such a spirit of nationalism in this small nation that even independence was not enough. The challenge became a religious crusade that motivated them to build boats and do battle with the Moors in North Africa. Success did not motivate them to return home but instead created an adventurous challenge—to explore the coast of Africa—as well as an economic challenge to gain a trade route to the East.

In the following decades they found their way to India and enjoyed a sixtyfold return on their investment. Italy and the Renaissance were now to be overshadowed by the spirit of the Portuguese and those who accepted the challenge she had created.

The initiative would swing next to Spain, France, and England; but Portugal was always there. Magellan started the first voyage around the world and new colonies were founded. Gradually the Portuguese became wealthy and then, almost as suddenly, they began to decline—until they were once again just a tiny nation alongside Spain. As the years passed, the children inherited the wealth but not the challenge; Portugal became a weak nation, sitting on the sidelines of history, watching the rise of others.

This was the single ingredient: to inherit the challenge caused growth, inheriting only the wealth caused collapse. Thus the key word becomes *challenge*. If there is no challenge, there is no need to strive except for more comfort. Yet to be comfortable to the exclusion of personal development is to preclude your ever gaining a sense of your own worth. If you appreciate the fact that you are capable of great success, comfort must not become so important as to destroy the challenge to grow and achieve.

As an example, in the 1950s the American space program was scheduled to .place a man on the moon by the year 2000. That changed with one word, *challenge*—the challenge of the first Russian Sputnik. The dynamic factors that determined the success of our space program are a dramatic illustration of the power of the concepts presented in this book. The program began with the greatest motivating need: pride in ourselves. This need could be satisfied only if we proved how capable we were, and this meant we *had* to win. In another respect, it meant the development, as a nation, of a positive self-image. To gain this positive self-image demanded that we achieve the victory.

Nevertheless these needs, by themselves, could not begin the process until they were activated by one catalytic ingredient, and that key factor was expectations. In other words, we had to believe that we as a nation deserved to be the first to the moon because we were the best. If it was within our potential, we were supposed to win. This belief triggered the needs for achievement, identity, and pride, which generated a powerful desire to set and achieve the goal.

Once the goal was set, the techniques discussed in this text were applied. A total commitment was made. We applied the acceptance-span technique, began at the point we believed possible, and went from there. We committed ourselves to the world. We sold ourselves on the benefits to be derived, and equally we created fear by realizing what the disadvantages would be if we did not win. We sold ourselves on those of our strengths that proved we should succeed.

Perhaps most important, we had the ability to fail. In those first efforts we watched our initial rockets abort in flight. When we seemed within range of success, on January 27, 1967, fire swept through a rocket and took the lives of Lt. Col. Virgil I. Grissom, Lt. Col. Edward H. White, and Lt. Comm. Roger B. Chaffee. With the deaths of these three astronauts, the goal of 1969 seemed out of reach; but the shock of failure reminds us that great achievements often require suffering. It is the same with the individual: the further he goes, the greater the risk. The more he gains, the more he can lose.

The triumph of Apollo 11 lies not in its achievement but in the symbol of its victory. It sets the standards of what we really can accomplish. If, in our success, we become complacent, we have sown the seeds of tomorrow's crisis. The same applies to you. If success causes you to rest, you may watch the world pass you by. Aggressive young men may catch you and inflation may steal your wealth.

Do you think that nothing succeeds like success? Then examine the rise and fall of nations, companies, institutions, and individuals. As they begin to succeed, they become satisfied. The satisfaction all too often leads to apathy, which culminates in obsolescence and eventual collapse. Watch as a sports team celebrates its victory and realize that at the same moment many embittered people are plotting their overthrow and defeat.

Success can be dangerous if it results in satisfaction, apathy, obsolescence, and defeat. It can be dangerous if it results in a loss of challenge. Try a different thought. Nothing succeeds like failure. If, when we fail, we are challenged to overcome the defeat and strive for victory to regain the challenge, then maybe *failure is what we need*. I am not suggesting that we enjoy failure or seek it. I am stating that your concern should not be with failure or success as much as it should be with the belief in yourself and your belief that you deserve to succeed. The challenge must always be with you. *Nothing succeeds like a challenge.* As Vince Lombardi used to say, "The Packers always win. It is just that sometimes the clock runs out on us."

Whether it is Portugal striving to defeat the Moors or to reach a new world or America striving for victory in World War II or to reach the moon, the common denominator is the same. Accept the challenge. Believe in yourself and in the fact that you deserve to grow and achieve continuously. Accept the challenge and be prepared to handle failure, rejection, and anxiety in the process of succeeding.

Your responsibility is clearly dramatized by the story of a boy who was determined to trick a wise old man who was known to have the answers to all questions. The boy caught a bird and, holding it in his hand behind his back, he came to the old man and asked: "Old man, what do I have in my hand?"

The all-knowing man answered: "A bird, my son."

Now the boy knew the old man would succeed in the first question, but he planned to catch him on the second question. He would ask him, "Is the bird dead or alive?" Now if the old man said it was dead, he would let it go; and if he said it was alive, he would crush it and show it dead. So he asked him, "Old man, is the bird dead or alive?"

The old man replied: "My son, that life is in your hands."

You are the boy, and the bird is your life—to do with as you wish. There is no longer anyone to force you to succeed. No teachers, parents, drill sergeants, or coaches. Just you. If you will be honest with yourself, you are ready to begin. Dream great dreams, and do not be afraid to fail while converting your dreams into realities.

INDEX

Acceptance, see Recognition
Acceptance span, 101, 159, 160, 201
Achieve, 16, 17, 20, 82, 188, 190, 191, 200, 201
Acting as if, 105, 106, 114, 115
Action, 151-153, 177
Advertising, 153, 155, 164, 167, 171, 177
Aggressive, 159, 191
Alpha level, 117-130, 131-139
American Motors, 163
Anxiety, 33-43, 81-85, 102, 103, 107, 111, 112, 118, 141, 167, 169, 178, 192, 202
Apollo II, 1, 201
Aristotle, 63
Assume consent, 183
Atomic energy, 10
Attention, 151, 152, 159, 160, 194, 195
Attitudes toward failure, 23-32
Authority, 178, 180, 191, 194
Awareness, 155, 156

Barracuda, 71, 72
Beer, 166
Benefits, 90, 104, 201
Benefits (sales), 170, 183-185, 188, 194
Body language, 158
Brain cells, 62
Brown, Charlie, 53

Capp, Andy, 31
Carey, Max, 29
Cars, 162-164, 169, 170
Chaffee, Lt. Comm. Roger B., 201
Challenge, 200, 202
Challenge thinking, 97, 98, 113
Change, 59-61, 101, 103, 104
Charisma, 53, 159

Charlie Brown, 53
Chrysler, 163
Cigarettes, 164
Closing, 102, 171, 185
Cobb, Ty, 29
Color Research Institute, 165
Comfortable, 59-61, 167, 170
Commitment to others, 103, 104, 114, 201
Competence, 176
Competition, 104, 105, 114
Composure, 48, 83, 159
Computers, 164, 180
Confidence, 13, 82
Confidence game, 47, 56
Conflict, 39-43, 167
Consent, assume, 183
Consumer motivation, 161-168
Control oriented, 53, 79, 80-81, 83, 97, 141-150, 156, 173, 174, 178-180, 194, 197
Creative energy, 33-43, 82, 88, 89, 111, 141, 189, 192
Criteria selling, 173
Criticism, 147, 148
Cunningham, Glen, 98

Demara, Ferdinand Walpo, 65-67
De-motivation, 19-22, 97, 161
Depression, 33-43, 81, 102, 107, 141, 167, 193
Descriptive technique, 89, 111, 148
Desire, 11, 12
Desire (consumer), 151, 152, 196, 197
Detergent, 165, 166
Dreams, 117

Ego defense mechanisms, 45-56, 81-84, 92, 93, 124, 125, 142, 143, 168, 172, 177, 179, 191

Einstein, 10
Electroencephalogram machine, 117
Empathy, 46-54, 157, 177
Engineers, 92
Enthusiasm, 47, 48, 159, 176
Exaggeration, 106, 107, 115
Expectations, 37-39, 93, 201
Express response, 180

FABR, 169, 171, 185, 197
Failure, 13-15, 20-22, 23-32, 90, 91,
    93-95, 102, 107, 111, 177, 185, 188,
    189-192, 201, 202
Fear technique, 90, 112, 201
Ford, 163
Fosbury, Dick, 92
Frankl, Dr., 64

General Motors, 163
Giving of yourself, 183
Gleem, 167
Goal oriented, 12
GOYA, 107, 108, 115
Great Imposter, 65-67
Grissom, Lt. Col. Virgil I., 201

Hawthorne study, 157, 193
Hidden persuaders, 166
Hippy culture, 60
Hitler, Adolf, 67
Honesty technique, 92
Hostility, 33-43, 141, 156, 157, 167,
    193, 195
Humor, 31, 105, 157, 159, 175, 177
Hypnosis, 59, 62, 88, 91, 117-130,
    131-139, 177

IBM, 28
Identity, 18, 78, 79, 201
Image matching, 164, 165, 170
Image projection, 142, 157-159, 165,
    173, 174, 175, 177, 178, 180, 194,
    195
Incentive technique, 89, 112
Interest, 151, 152, 155, 156, 179, 180

Jogging, 102, 103, 104

Kennedy, Jack, 159
Kitty Hawk, 1
Knowledge, 12, 13

Laser beam, 91
Leadership, 104, 114, 187-198
Learning process, 24-27
Life insurance, 24-27, 88, 153, 159,
    160, 164, 168, 171, 172, 180, 184,
    193
Life Science Library, 67
Lucy, 53

Magellan, 200
Money, 89, 196
Moses, Grandma, 63
Motivation, 15-19, 20, 83, 161, 174,
    197

Need-satisfaction, 152
Needs, 15-20, 103, 161
Nice guy game, 46, 47, 81, 82, 171,
    191
Non-verbal communication, 158

Objections, 157, 170, 172, 173, 184,
    185, 190, 191, 192, 197
Obstacle conversion, 98, 99, 113
Obstacle technique, 92, 113
Olympics, 1968, 92
One-to-one, 53, 141-146, 156, 173,
    174, 178, 198
Outer Symbols, 108, 109, 115
Oyster, 98

Packard, Vance, 166
Pavlov, 153
Pearl, 98
Pecking order, 178, 179, 185
Persuasion, 169-187, 192, 195-197
Peter Principle, 38, 188, 190
Pheidippides, 11
Portugal, 200, 202
Positive affirmations, 88, 111, 128,
    129
Positive thinking, 97, 113
Potential, 61-68, 71-73, 187, 201
Presenting solutions, 167, 169, 174,
    176, 185, 193, 196-197
Pride, 201
Problems (consumer needs), 169,
    170, 171, 172, 174, 176, 180, 185,
    195-196
Prospecting, 102, 104-105, 153-157

Psychology Today, 121
Punishment, 109, 116

Questioning techniques, 161, 172-173, 180-181, 183-185

Rapport, 96, 151-160, 161, 169, 174, 175, 179, 180, 185, 192-195
Real estate sales, 51, 153, 161, 164, 165, 168, 193
Recognition, 17-20, 80, 81, 83, 95, 101, 146, 170, 171, 174, 182, 189, 194, 195
Rejection, 19, 20, 25-32, 35, 36, 81, 83, 95, 96, 98, 99, 103, 142, 143, 146, 147, 170, 171, 174, 177, 188, 190, 194, 198
Repetition, 109, 110
Repressed thoughts, 123, 127
Reward, 109, 115, 116
Roosevelt, Theodore, 32
Ruth, Babe, 29, 61

Sanders, Col., 63, 64
Salesmanship, 151-160, 161-168, 169-174, 186
Satisfaction, 170, 171, 173, 174, 176, 197, 198
Self-acceptance, 18, 20, 149, 182
Self competition, 103, 105, 114
Self image, 57-68, 69-75, 84, 96, 97, 99, 108, 118, 148, 189, 192, 195
Self-sufficient, 79, 80, 82, 83, 189, 190
Sensitivity, 145-147, 157, 158, 159, 160, 175, 177
Sentence completion, 181, 185
Series of decisions, 152-158
Skeels, Dr. Harold M., 72, 73
Smoking, 88, 102
Sputnik, 200
Stockbroker, 30, 36, 154, 160, 162, 164
Strength bombardment, 95-97, 113, 201
Subservient, 192
Sympathy, 148, 149, 159, 175, 182, 193, 198
Sympathy note, 156

Tailored technique, 102, 113
Techniques of persuasion, 175-186
Territorial infringement, 176, 177
Toothpaste, 166
Total commitment, 90, 91, 112, 201
Transcendental meditation, 118

Values, 78, 103, 136
Vivid imagination, 112, 129

White, Lt. Col. Edward H., 201
Wright Brothers, 1

NOTES

NOTES

NOTES

NOTES

NOTES

NOTES

NOTES

NOTES

NOTES

NOTES

NOTES

NOTES